EVIL TRAN

RUSSELL RUSSELL

Copyright © 2024 Russell Russell

All rights reserved. No portion of this Book may be reproduced in any form without permission from the author/publisher. This book may not be lent, resold without the prior written permission from the author/publisher.

Table of Contents

CHAPTER 1
Social Oppression   5

CHAPTER 2
Three Evils   27

CHAPTER 3
Showers with the Other Sex   67

CHAPTER 4
Obey Trans   76

CHAPTER 5
Biology Does Not Count   90

CHAPTER 6
Harry Potter and the Trans Triangle Argument   117

CHAPTER 7
How to Stop Cancel Culture   136

CHAPTER 8
Goodbye   153

CHAPTER 9
A Transformative Tale for 6 Year Olds   166

Glossary   172

Chapter 1

Social Oppression

I write this for UK citizens in the hope they wise up and alter the greatest mistake of modern society since Hitler was supported in his murderous actions to gas people to death.

The only difference between the world-war German ideology and Evil Tran is that Hitler could only take lives. Those victims did not lose their sense of freedom to know the truth that evil was being perpetuated upon them; they were not embroiled in a brainwashing cultural scheme where fiction becomes fact, such as the claim that men who identify as women are women and that it must be true because parliament passed a law. That is the underlying logic behind Evil Tran's privileged social position. 'We' say it, you believe it, or else there will be trouble for you if you publicly speak out against our views. We will charge you with hate speech or cancel you.

Evil Tran is the term I use more or less to explain how transgender ideology and its vocal exponents contribute to a social evil whereby the human essence is undermined by what might be called oppressive intellectual forces found in public and private organisations like the media, health, and education services.

Their collective views, implemented through guidelines and stipulations, create control over workers, limiting freedoms of speech and blocking the natural flow of expressions people like to feel as an emotional soul. Today, if any individual says an inappropriate thing, according to an organisation's interpretation of UK values, an employee will be sacked or reprimanded by a manager whose main guideline is to represent the organisation as consumer-friendly, progressive, and a modern outfit that supports minority rights.

These organisations publicly sound as if they are moral, loving, and caring toward all minorities, which is genuinely nice to hear for everyone, but this value scheme is not always being expressed fairly and squarely, whereby it is true to the logic inherently held within most society members. In other words, an organisation has to represent fairly and consistently in accordance with understanding fuller society and the members found there; if not, you simply choose a blanket response (to create a good media public relations image) that in turn victimizes workers from being represented with their access to human rights, as for example in the Maya Forstater case. She lost her job for speaking her mind on social media. Once society starts and lives in this sort of malarkey, we find ourselves sinking into a Nazi prejudicial state where the elites dictate societal norms and insist on reprogramming our intellectual thinking and commenting.

This book is not just about trans issues in conflict with society (per se) but about the rights of society to define for itself values that rise above the human rights argument to support the trans minority at the expense of the majority values found within UK society. Anyone arguing against me here overall for the points I make is arguing for the undermining of the majority, which has no logical basis given we exist in the modern era with protections for all minorities anyway.

If we lose the social norms and rights to voice our opinions, we take democracy backwards in time. Maya Forstater lost her job for upholding the view that biological men cannot be women. To cancel people for holding an honest, fair opinion is draconian authoritarian and speculative of the law, where Forstater eventually got compensated thousands of pounds by the High Courts. She is a telling example of where the average UK citizen finds themselves in relation to where they work. Shut up or else, culture.

What I explain here argues for a referendum so that people can take back what is a natural human right to define what a woman and man are. We are being overpowered by an academic minority that supports a medical human rights argument and a social philosophy that politicians support. They have argued, very successfully, that the mental construct humans use to define the self can include the idea that we can self-identify as the opposite sex. They cling to the term gender but then inform us they are women establishing a social logic of two possibilities. Once you self ID you become that sex, the biological male or female no longer counts – it is only the self-identity you proclaim that is male or female. This is fine if we all agreed to these unusual terms and conditions or that science had conclusively made a mistake in principle to attribute gender at birth.

They say things like that men can be women because women are socially constructed, or have certain psychological aspects that men can characteristically show themselves to possess and hence are women. For this to stand society has to agree that women are shaped predominantly as a definition around behaviour and not biology, so it can then be argued intellectually and academically that a man can mould himself into that form.

The Evil Tran Brigade reshapes logic into a working platform from which to act. They have the point of view that some men are born and grow psychologically as women. This relies totally on accepting that this psychic aspect is all there is to a woman. In order for this definition of a woman to stand legitimately, society has to reject any connection to the biological status of a woman, which obviously must include womb, sex eggs and the ability to give birth.

I say men cannot be women because women have always been known as a physically identified thing strictly connected to biological aspects that men cannot access, like giving birth. If biology on its own does not make a woman the biology counts to discount men from being women.

So who is right? What makes it right?

Politicians had no right whatsoever to cross this line of natural logic we all uphold, which carries a biological understanding carried through the history of the human race that all our ancestors, like us today, could clearly identify, via physical aspects, the man from the woman for mating or partner purposes. Introducing a confusing fresh set of political ideas, that we have to concede to, involves the identification of the woman via a claim from the person making the claim that they are a woman, sometimes they argue that men have the appropriate psychological aspects to inform us who is a woman. Both principles of argument have one resounding weak spot that is a discredit to the political parties who passed the law. They have not understood that they had to prove to themselves that a woman has no physical part in her existence. If, in the meantime, society can prove and argue that women do have a specific biological difference in defining themselves from men, then it literally becomes impossible for men to be women based upon that understanding and argument that men simply do not possess a DNA chromosome action that produces a womb and the ability to give birth. We cannot escape this value to define women unless we ignore it as unimportant compared to self-identity.

When there are flukes of nature with exotic mismatches of chromosomes, then the weirdest of things can manifest where a human can almost be a half woman and half man, but these extremely rare examples do not alter the majority example whereby men cannot give birth.

The transgender group does not fit outside the general rule that men have X-Y chromosomes and women have X-X. Understood, a biologist would laugh at you for suggesting that a biological man can be a woman because it is impossible to literally change sex as an adult once your sex has been established via your DNA historical activity. And added to this, the main trans argument is that they can change to what they want anyway, so whatever they are biologically can be ignored is their message. They do not propose as their key principle argument that they are genuinely a biological fit to their identity, but it suits some trans arguers to argue from all places of argument. The thing to note is that the new woman, the trans woman, is achieved by anyone who says they are a woman; the biology is not the matter of concern. So what we are arguing against is whether some man can become a woman because he says he wishes to be known as a woman. Biology does not count as an argument of real relevance here; it is the ability to choose your gender that is real and in law, and what a trans woman is in principle. A true trans woman just says I can choose my identity, and I choose to be a woman. Beat that; you can't.

We cannot stop someone with that attitude and conviction from standing by their rights. But we have to agree on how we will treat them and how we perceive them. We agree to be polite and accept their personal ways, but should politicians have agreed they could be a legal fiction and be adorned with the same rights as women? Trans women exist in countries without official status as women and entry into personal women spaces. Should trans people expect that we all perceive them as women if clearly we do not? How can we process what we see as male into a female? And believe to ourselves that person is actually female?

Having the right to identify as a woman (in a way that normal men do not) seems fair. We cannot expect all people to be the same. But just because they see themselves as women and we allow that right, or cannot stop it, that does not mean we have to agree they are actually women. The two principles do not come joined at the hip of logic. We should not alter what we think a woman is just because men say they are women also. We should stick to what we believe. And we categorically do not believe a man can be a woman. Strictly speaking politicians ask that we treat transwomen for all intents and purposes as if women. They do not clarify with objective values that some men are actually women, but nor do they make clear that some men are not women. Meanwhile society muddles along where many people in the media, education, or political spheres argue that trans women are real women.

As soon as this red line of logic is crossed by an extreme minority dictating the agenda, they have to be challenged. You have the duty to defend what a man and woman are because your view and how you arrive at it are part of you. Trans activists, academics, and politicians attempt to take that part of you and reorder it as if they are rightfully correcting us all. An obscene insistence. For them, a man is a woman, and a woman is a man if any human suddenly identifies as so. Such a moral and logical failing is the beginning of a momentous change for society that will set us back into the dark ages where we took orders from royalty as a way forward. This modern-day ruling is being perpetuated by the academic (royal) PhD classes with fancy rhetoric and authoritative manners. They are rearranging a core belief, value system, and innate biological understanding, whereby they are dictating to us and rewiring our thought process via the media and especially the education classes for students of all ages. They are signalling, arguing, and ordering via UK law that, firstly, men can be women as a fact about reality, whereas in the details of this truth, men are women if those men identify as women. This reality of theirs is actually only proven to exist in political reality; it has zero bearing on biological proof that biological men can be women, and again, a failing in the reality of everyday life in terms of what general society believes: we reject the idea men in dresses are women.

Once society attempts to fiddle with and alter this natural inclination and drive, it is a recipe for conflict because eventually people realize they cannot naturally process information as political powers insist. Understood, the mood and feeling become toxic from what is a strongly felt insult occurring from this unbelievable situation, where a collective of people are ordering the rest of us how to conceive an obvious traditional objective reality; that has been argued away and cleverly managed, instating that woman is a purely subjective opinion. This alternative perception undermines traditional-held views and has become an objective fact. Understood in this way, some of us feel a type of hatred or outrageousness at the situation, while meanwhile, people who see it the gender identity way disagree to our traditional conception of a woman and feel equally outraged and hateful. Both sides feel they know the real truth and hold the objective facts that decide the matter.

This self ID principle of expressing the self has become a modern-day freedom and power for the individual rights of any human. It is quite spectacular and has been galvanized by the youth elements at university who have been educated and mentored in context to the academic and social implications. But amazingly, there is one resounding lost insight that everyone discounts and forgets, and that is that society in general decides these sort of universal principles such as who is a man and who is a woman, what is evil and what is not, when should we laugh or cry, get angry and speak our minds, show our feelings, and be real human beings, not some corporate university method that teaches us a manufactured ideal. Where the powers involved in corporations are about a way of maximizing work forces and public relations for profits, while academics deal in the currency of influence via intellectual content.

What a woman is or a man, is not decided by a few people with academic political credentials, as ironically it has been. And that is why there must be a referendum to decide the issue so that people in society decide who is a man and who is a woman, not some modern-day elitist scheme and arrogant display from politicians and academics who often between them work in unison via think tanks or advisory panels and are without doubt armed and extremely dangerous, as shows with various examples like their handling of COVID, climate change reforms, artificial intelligence, and wars. Those areas involve specialist knowledge, expert arguments, and political decision-making. What a man and woman are does not involve the need for any expert from any quarter, unless, of course, you are one of those modern-day people who believe in subordination driven by the educated and political classes because they know best. Most kids at university are groomed to this structural common sense.

How can anyone inform us that some of the women (men might have sex with) can technically become men? How can anyone tell a woman that the man they might have sex with might actually be a woman? It is a ludicrous assumption to make from a few arguing the way they do for gender identity that they have the right to tell each of us how we define and decide what a woman is. It is a deplorable thing to alter and insist we do so without our collective vote on the issue; this has not been decided scientifically but as a human rights issue. When understood exactly what a man and woman are as a definition, it is a society decision to make, not a political decision. Hence, we need a referendum, not a dictatorship of misleading logic and acts of bullying upon every citizen that we have to alter our thinking and do as we are being told or else face consequences.

The real consequences are not that women have to shower with men or that kids can take puberty blockers and hormone replacement aids to alter some aspect of their natural biology. No, the real issue and consequence is that we will have to live with the oppressive ideology that men are women and, in turn, live with people who really believe such a claim as if it is logically correct actually true and we should all agree. Why would we agree to a fraudulent claim from sickly sycophantic people and then socially express ourselves as agreeing when we do not? And the answer is that we won't agree to the fraudulent claim, but we might well shut up just to fit in at work or with who we socialize. Or if a broadcaster, newspaper writer, celebrity, and so forth, have to weigh the social reaction of the group we are reliant upon, this means lying and modifying what truth to state or not state. Get it wrong, you will get cancelled from work contracts and positive social following.

It stands as one of the greatest insults and miscarriages to what democratic society really is – a system made on votes and understanding of what a majority of people represent and want. If we cannot have a referendum about the very method by which we define a woman, then it means suddenly that the state decides how we must think and perceive reality itself. They are basically telling us that the real way to determine a woman is through a psychological trait of self-knowledge, which is merely a bizarre opinion about sexual identity. And that, therefore, what we decide using our eyes and brains as we project a natural analysis upon a woman or man is inaccurate, unreliable, out of date, and then the coup de grâce – immoral and against the human rights of a minority group called transgenders.

Added to the political stance, corporate power plays express themselves whereby organisations suggest new collective ways they should react and relate to anyone questioning the narrative, while also virtue-signalling to us all as to how we should behave as decent ordinary citizens. A remarkable liftoff as we see the modern-day ascension of public and private organisations setting the example that we should follow their lead in the display of supporting human rights. Suddenly we are swept into embracing a mindfulness and a moral reality whereby it is right and logical to accept the everyday condition that men can be women if men say so.

This perspective totally overlooks our natural inclinations to decide for ourselves or that we should even decide the matter! Which for me is the greatest modern day sin of modern times (in the UK) which if we allow to continue means the compressing of the human individual and the expanding of the collective state I call Evil Tran upon the individual ordering us to behave to their collective moral fibre which I will remind you again totally ignores our rights to decide for ourselves how to conduct our sensory natures in relation to one of our prime sexual sensory drives – to know the difference between men and women for purposes that relate to reproduction of species, sensory self-gratification, and a simple everyday way to distinguish women from men for practical purposes. All of which were our rights as humans through 300 hundred thousand years of Homo Sapient history. Suddenly, all of that has been stolen away from us, and amazingly, in a category we would have thought was safe from a redistribution of logic. Suddenly, freedom becomes like a communist or Nazi oppression, ordering us what to do from the political, corporate, and media dimensions of social reality. The UK is entering into a political democratic climate like Iran, China, or some other lesser democracy where the state decides, or else.

In short, if you stand by the Evil Tran phenomenon, you do not realize all the oppressive sanctions you are helping to impose on the natural freedoms of individuals. Yes, whoever you are, have the right to see it all your own way, but so do we, the vast majority, which means (in relation to what a man or a woman is) we have the duty and right as a sophisticated society to decide by referendum vote and not assume wrongly that the matter has been decided by a few thousand activists and a few hundred politicians; that is not democracy.

A large faction within elite society keeps coming down heavy and threatening when we do not concede to their ideologies. Meanwhile, most people are not aware of this situation because, on a daily basis, they are not generally experiencing this forced order. It is there as a middle class structure battering anyone of position who speaks out for the majority of citizens found in an expanding set of rules and regulations set by government and proxy agents like major corporate organisations who set limits to workers freedoms around content of speech. If you do not limit your personal expressions, you will be sacked for not fitting their organisational scheme to look consumer-friendly by being politically correct.

The worker has become an agent of corporate and public image for the good of political values around human rights and other rationalized ideals, which in turn seeks favour from the stormy youth, especially via university systems where they learn to be fair for all and hence love it when a company explains via virtue signalling how they represent the values of tomorrow and progression towards that aim. This means bullying and threatening workers via guidelines that are quite simply a book of commandments that include intolerance towards anyone voicing any criticism around trans issues that affect general society. If voiced, these organisations believe you are going against trans peoples' human rights to exist free from victimization, which is the general tone and feel for their dimension of truth.

Understood in a fuller context, major corporations are upholding an oppressive, regimented process put into place by lawyers limiting freedoms of speech, which they have no right to do just because they are managing to do so without technically breaking the law or even making it explicitly clear within their stipulations as to what you should or should not say, as seen as victimizing trans people. They would rather make it clear to the public in their declarations that they are all inclusive and treat all people equally, leaving it to our imaginations as to what the red lines are that we as workers cannot overstep, like saying men cannot be women. A plausible consideration to make, and then voice in conversation on social media, especially at the biological level of logic, which incidentally is how we have always determined who is a woman or man.

Start to make a stand now, or lose your soul stifled and forced into silence to accept that a man is a woman, or else face punishment as what the Labour Party proposes to send people to prison for purposely misgendering someone; they mean it in a context like when relating to a trans woman as if 'she' is a man. Which by the way 'she' is a biological man. Yes, like me, you might be polite and address the person as Miss, but what if a person is not clearly a trans woman but identifies as one? Then, like me, you will probably address him as Mister or as a clear man, and then the guy might get distressed and upset and argue to you that you have misgendered him and remind you that it is a police matter or that he will tell your corporate bosses. Ironically, if a trans woman were misgendered it would be an act of misogyny because he is a woman in law. So technically I just committed a crime against the Orwellian state for purposely using he instead of she. If the person is non-binary they would be upset for addressing them as he or she! Or they would insist to be known as he and she or some other complicated transgender etiquette.

How can you sit in a pub in a social group and know if the man opposite, whom you refer to as mate, is not going to be offended by assuming he is a man if he is a trans woman? He doesn't have to wear a dress to be a legal woman, so suddenly you would be trapped in a legal maze where, if your sensitivity is numbed by alcohol, you might refer to him definitively incorrect in accordance with the law and new social norms and find yourself arrested for misgendering.

I call them trannies for in this book or men in dresses to create an exact image in mind. This is not actually the right term you should use socially in conversation with others, as it arguably whacks of disrespect, but is not misgendering because a tranny is a man who cross dresses like the comedian Lily Savage, a transvestite similar to a drag queen. Often, such people do not claim transgender status, but because many of them do – then for me a tranny is a trans person.

The world cannot be run on exact formality and precise information terms, especially in social interactions with others, because each of us would have to learn a thousand different rules, social norms, and organisational guidelines. What we state in conversation must hold flexible boundaries, or otherwise uneducated people or non-academic people who do not read or are not sponges for information cannot keep up with these sort of insisted for changes by the academic classes supporting causes that might mean something to them, especially when being paid officially to represent a certain group, but mean zero to people like myself. How many laws am I supposed to know? Shall I sit practicing daily learning and memorizing them all?

I only came to learn about trans issues by absolute chance in relation to JK Rowling (the Harry Potter writer) who got involved in all this trans stuff due to supporting a woman who lost her job called Maya Forstater. Suddenly I have been sucked into a toxic battleground where slippery, emotionally violent students roam to intimidate anyone who stands against the idea that a man can be a woman. They are backed up by a woke politically correct elite gang culture, a mob normally well versed in what seems media-friendly and of use for public relations in education, politics, health services, the press and television broadcasters, government, public, and international companies, especially. They are all on the public relations angle, with an acute understanding of what policy boosts profits indirectly via virtue signalling, be it genuinely endorsed or not.

I choose to be a bit edgy in my choice of rhetoric and language and not have to keep referring to specialist Stonewall dictionaries for guidance on how to refer to trans people. There are too many up-and-coming instances from the tranny academic state about what words are appropriate or not. I find this an obscene insistence that I literally would have to learn twenty new words in order to know what I am saying is specific enough not to offend anyone in the trans world, as if some queen or king or official organisation, plus some trans women, as they call themselves, are not really transgender in genuine spirit but rather a copycat trend where for their own university social cool, they start to dress a bit feminine and claim trans status. I cannot imagine how such cross-dressing is trendy, but then again, superstars like Brad Pitt indulge in cross-dressing. Such a kind is arguably closer to being a tranny (not that they know it) than many people who identify as women. The reason I say this is that this is not an exact science to qualify as trans; it is very obscure what entry points one needs socially to qualify as trans. But as a guiding rule of thumb, it specifically involves a conscious reflection that you are identifying as a woman if you happen to be a biological man. Brad Pitt does not identify as such and hence is not transgender, but I can assure you that he may well have ten more attributes of feminine behaviour that a self-confessed trans person does not, so objectively may well be more of a trans person by those characteristics. Will we, as a social group, make that distinction and tell our friends that we think another friend of ours is a trans person but he does not know it? We might call it pre trans.

Within all the confusing red lines to social behaviour, which might upset different factions, is a mindfield that shadows people in a dark, threatening way, pushing for oversensitive social etiquettes while at the same time enjoying the freedom to be brazen and disrespectful to any cisgender or even transgender that does not support the official narratives of organisations like Stonewall.

Please note for the record that if you were to address someone as a tranny who is transgender, that might get you arrested for hate speech, even though you could plead ignorance. Police could technically arrest and charge you depending on how they view the matter. The argument and defence are that you are using a slang term to mean a specific thing, and transgender or trans is not far from tranny as a colloquial term. Just be certain that members of society will have to be careful in the future in the UK and USA, as eventually these situations will play out.

If I was a tranny and felt hurt by you calling me mister, then why should I not complain officially to the police if the law says I am protected from being misgendered? I do not encourage anyone to follow my manners or even my logic on all occasions, as logic can be a personal choice in relation to how we personally think or how we prefer to favour certain standards of dealing with something. Often we merely choose logic that expresses our character or personality. Do we go to the local shop at greater expense to save time or visit the supermarket a distance away to save money? It depends on your mood and circumstances, but there is logic in both decisions, normally around what is best in some way. If you have a well-paid corporate job, tighten your anti-trans views; otherwise, you might lose that job. I do not encourage suicide missions at the expense of your livelihood, but maybe if we ever get a bigger-sounding gang, you might consider voicing your opinion, even if via a false identity on a social media platform. Many people find public commenting, which causes arguments, a deflating experience and prefer to avoid contentious issues.

I can only assure you that, from both sides of the trans argument, we would be a stronger society for holding a referendum on the matter. But that said, I genuinely believe they would lose all rights to enter any women's spaces, so logically, why would a trans person work towards a referendum? They gained access to toilets and showers a long time ago. There would not be anything more to be gained. So it is logical for them to argue against my view, but on a scale of honesty, integrity, and decency towards society members, a trans person should want to know what people wish for their country. Many trans people would never enter the (opposite biological sex) shower rooms and subject people there to having to shower next to them. But that is not the point, because when society makes laws, rules, and regulations, we as citizens are forced to concede our wills to those rules or be conscious of them in a way we reflect and regard them. I can assure you that women showering naked at a gym do not wish a man to shower next to them, and once forced to accept this rule, they are being oppressed at a psychological and emotional level. It is the very principle that is obscene unless we agree to it, which fundamentally we do not. But that does not mean to say that the differences in opinions around toilet use are decidedly greater in one view or the other, given certain polls. So at closer inspection of some issues, be that a man really can be a woman or not in law, society members might agree trans people can use whatever toilets they wish anyway.

The real issue here is not just spaces that belong to women but the rights of people to decide what a woman and a man are. Take that right away, which it has been, then we allow powers to politicians they were not made to have, and if they were meant to, they should then explain via parliamentary inquiry exactly why they made the decisions they did. They would have to explain why the biological aspect of womanhood has no bearing on their decision-making process. What experts proved to them: biology does not count. Does this political killer of women possess magical authoritarian powers, giving them the right to reprogram the whole of the human race with how they conceive and perceive women to be; as an entity without a womb or ability to give birth? Should we all be thankful that people more intelligent than ourselves have taken the time to reorder us for best purposes based on their best intentions? No, we should kill this academic bullying know-it-all political scheme before it invades all aspects of our lives, stopping us from choosing as we see fit. If not, they will quite literally take over our lives via a myriad of rules and regulations, orders, and stipulations; an insidious bureaucracy where they stamp us as progressive citizens.

I do not exactly stand with any particular group in all their debates against transgender people due to the diversity and richness of my opinions. I do not care that men can self-identify as a woman; but I object that they can be classified as if literally a woman. It makes no sense to me and the culture I was brought up in, or how my brain clarifies to itself who are men and who are women when I see them. Some women's groups against self-identification would not agree with my exact take on the issue because I do not care a person can self identify I merely care about the definition of a woman to be biologically defined from which we would cancel men being classified as women. However, such groups would agree we should have a referendum, as that would solve the issue as a fair way for society to be structured by its citizens. If not, they will commit the same sin as the trans activists and lobbyists, which is to make pleas to politicians to alter laws via lobbyist arguments, which excludes general society and favours academics and organized powers with access to big money and intellectual influence, something I call corporate intellectualization.

Others would not agree to me calling trans women men in dresses or trannies, and so forth terms, as they like to be totally respectful and are lured by the presentation of appearing fair, respectful, decent, and orderly in an educated way. I use the term men in dresses to be informative and exact to create a mental image, whereas trans woman all too often makes one think it's a biological woman and that trans man is a biological man when in fact it is a woman who says she is a man. I only know this because I had to learn this stuff beforehand. I had no idea whether a trans woman meant a man in a dress or a woman acting as a man. Why would the average person know?

When I hear anyone, especially feminists, say they stand for trans rights with the proviso that they just do not agree to them being the opposite sex and entering women-only spaces, I just flutter my eyes and feel like saying – well so what, why even say it? We all, more or less, know to support anyone in the world so that they can feel free to represent themselves openly and freely and enjoy other privileges of freedom. It is an automatic, inherited, and agreed-upon principle we all forward without having to publicly state it.

Many people confuse the issue when supporting trans rights, wrongly believing that to question if a man is a woman, this goes against supporting trans rights. No, it does not stop you from supporting their rights to think they are women; they can still believe and act as they do, and others can agree with that aspect of their rights. But others like me do not agree with their belief that they are actually real women, and once so, it becomes almost automatically logical to disagree that they should have access to women's spaces. If the trans' community believes we should stop stating the truth as we see it, they are asking that we cease from being human in our use of thoughts that always naturally propagate, creating our understanding and sense of expressed free will. They have no right to ask that just because they are a minority or a law has been passed. We, the majority, have rights. Those rights are equal to those of any minority. Those rights include thoughts and feelings about transgender people that we find inconsistent with our own logic that a man cannot be a woman based on biology. The trans community needs to understand our problems with them, not just their problems with us. We have the right to restrict certain powers that any self-affirming group can exercise if we would not wish those powers for ourselves, like, for instance, entering opposite-sex spaces. They should not have greater powers than us, the majority, based on the twist of logic that these men wish to be treated as women.

The continual frame of argument and understanding from these people and their official organisations is as if all their problems are caused by our lack of understanding towards them. This is a false manipulative belief that merely acts to maintain a grip on influencing people's minds via its sloppy claim. The deeper truth is that many of the problems they have are well deserved because biology does actually count toward determining what a woman is. These people have little right to tell us that biology does not count. This fundamental idea is close to the understanding we all share as a value that our male or female biology is a unique power and remarkably different from the opposite sex. When reflected upon, we defend our right to maintain this value, and obviously this can cause the trans community pain, hurt, and suffering as we point blank inform them that we do not wish any men to be known as women because it insults our sensibilities. It's a tough stance, but one that has to be maintained and fought for – if not we allow a replacement of values, beliefs, and understanding to frame our own souls. The educational trans bullying scheme currently expressing itself through UK society is a method from the intellectual classes to instate and force changes inside our brains so that we think and behave to a classification of goodwill to all citizens to the degree we lie to ourselves that men can be women. Next, they might ask that all men buy a dress to show solidarity with all trans people and parade themselves on International Transgender Day wearing that dress. Not a bad way to show solidarity, but letting men into women only spaces forwards that support in a distasteful way and imposes a lot of testing of a female's sense of privacy as she stands naked before a stranger who is a biological man.

Strictly speaking, every man we meet now may well be a woman in his own mind, and hence, in law, is so to some degree. How do we deal with this new way? Do we feel comfortable with it? Personally, I feel awkward and oppressed that I would have to avoid misgendering someone for fear of reprisals. Further, I have no right to ask a man if he is a man or a woman, because I have no right to ask that of anyone anyway. In the case of the tranny, I would be insulting him by treating him differently by asking if he is a man or a woman, and from these circumstances, he can call the police or report me to my work superiors if I were to ask him in a way that he deemed inappropriate as if being victimized. In this sense, a minority has more rights than the majority, as the legal state of play in the UK. Socially, these events have yet to commonly unfold. We are being closed off from normal standards of freedom. We are being forced into social etiquettes against our liking so as not to upset half a percent of the UK (trans) population and its laws. All of this is part of Evil Tran. Many powers, such as the media, health, and education, signal to us that it is virtuous not to upset the minority transgender community. From which, again, some people alter their behaviour to suit these ideologies, like, for instance, not questioning if a man can use the gym female showers. At every change like this, there is always a new and developing minority, and we would have to alter our ways to suit them. Before we know it, all we will become is an entity swept into changes by all minority claims. This is not what humans are: that they compromise all free will to be themselves just because a minority claims it is selfish; we hold on to our own values, like, for instance, agreeing with the value that women should, in some instances, have protection from men entering their spaces, especially showers, toilets, and changing rooms.

Please note that many trannies, do not insist on using opposite-sex spaces. Such men (trans women) like to be thought of as feminine and treated as such, but probably realize they are not real women but a rare abnormality in between, where we can argue that a transwoman is a man who acts like a biological woman and may feel like a woman in emotions and feelings if such a category exists exclusively to women in theory. This has never been proven but is lauded about by the trans mob and counterargued by the feminist groups that men cannot feel like women. If so, then we can at least call them transwomen and lend them some credibility, as they sure as hell are not normal men or women, but people who say they are more of a woman in spirit than a man.

What they do not realize is that, grouped with political powers, corporate realities, nationalized organisations, university thinking, the media, and especially American celebrities, trans people hold an unlikely powerful position in relation to human rights that not only challenges society but is oppressing it, not just restructuring it. These collectives of elites are not progressing our world for the sake of the minority; they are undermining it at the stake of the majority. Most of them are well paid, have career successes, and are used to having high social standing and respect; they lead many others somewhat, and the term often used for them is elites.

It is one of the greatest intellectual deceits and liberties to have ever entwined itself through society: man is a woman if man says so. He can enter women spaces because politicians say so, backed by other elites.

Evil Tran is a strangulation machine, and it will suppress you into submission eventually as the social orders change to favour elites. I am a guy who believes only a referendum can save us from that fate. I believe in destroying the sanctions made by elites, and if you are one such elite – I promise you I am your enemy.

If you think you have the duty and right to tell people how they should deem a man or woman to be, then you are wrong to think that, and you should correct your error before you do damage to the souls of others. We, the people, have the right to choose as a collective state and define what we regard as a deeply meaningful concept called woman.

Chapter 2

Three Evils

If God is truth and exists, would God agree that a man can be a woman? And if God does not exist, then what in your own truth allows you to think a man is a woman if he says he is? Explain your guiding principle of logic. I bet you can't. In which case do you agree to this change of law in the UK, as if they are God ordering us? Do you really believe it is a collective truth? You probably just don't care, and I cannot blame you for just getting on with your own life and its problems. But it does mean by law that we could be either male or female to any person who meets us, whether we like it or not. Our outward bodily image does not count in law to decide our gender. Instead, it is rather an out of date concept with no power to maintain its position. If people were aware of this fact they might be alarmed that visual identity as a value is undermined by trans people and their political support.

What was a woman is now is only a possibility. To know you would need to ask her and she can in theory say she is a man – a trans man. In some logical sense, you are not allowed to make a visual distinction to guide you as to what a man or a woman is anymore because anyone can say they are the opposite gender to what they look like based on physical appearances, and once so, why then are you assuming them to be one particular gender? Any assumption could be an act of prejudice and also illogical because, socially, they are in principle a man, woman, or non-binary. However, what you really are also is someone who uses their brain power in a habitual, natural fashion to process information, like, for instance, people's faces and anatomy. This involves unconscious automatic processes that forward information, which presses you to create a conscious experience and decision for the next few moments of life. This is very important stuff, and all that it is to being human at its natural instinctive levels, where had we been any different, we may not have survived to be here. It is part of our intelligence and sense of spirit to formulate truth and define a reality that, if not coordinated correctly, creates a different outcome from what we expect or hope for. To coordinate correctly, we have chosen a method of honest arguing and inquiry where results can be remembered, compared, and quantified to establish the best way forward. At its most basic endeavour, this method allows us to taste a food or liquid and, through experience, decide whether it is enjoyable and valuable in some way or not. As humans developed through time, this memory recognition of what value a thing has for us was one of our building blocks to how we experience life, and recognizing humans as male and female was one of them. Yes, we need imagination to engineer a car or space rocket; we need expert brains to invent many things we find in advanced societies; but we do not need anyone to tell us how we process objects we see like other humans, and in that, we each know what a woman or man is because time and tradition have embedded it in our brain awareness systems as an exact value and meaning. Evil Tran wishes to destroy all of that.

When Evil Tran writes government guidelines it will advise us that it is best not to make assumptions based on dress codes and that it is best to act with discernment and tact when encountering someone. In other words proceed with caution in a natural setting we have encountered thousands of times. If it were not to advise that, it would leave UK citizens in a continued state of conflict, similar to a highway code that does not advise a driver when to wait and give way to another driver, like at a junction. The social order would be stumped. Just because we do not receive government advice in this official way via email or through the post telling us about what would be called codes of conduct does not mean it is not being upheld via direct or indirect means through the press, television news, organisational guidelines, law, and enforcement where police have to sometimes judge criticism of the trans community in the context of whether it could be termed hate speech.

So what we have is a current of activity made up of individual pathways informing and adjusting us via acts of information that draw conclusions and produce standards of behaviour in our individual brains. All of which becomes copied or reassembled to help form a collective society in its social norms. This overall process equates to adjustments within society and our own individual awareness and understanding, where we are encouraged to regard tolerance for others and what they want as a good moral quality to uphold. Hence, gay people can get married or foster children, and society believes this to be fair when, sixty years ago, society in general would have thought this wrong.

You probably think that you yourself would never be so unfair and prejudiced had you lived back then, but I beg to differ, the USA in the 1960s was indulging in a culture where black people were segregated from whites, so do not assume the whole country was in uproar about the unfairness of it all. They just fell into place following what was happening around them while some black people and some students of all colours fought the racist indoctrinate. These sorts of values do not get changed without governments taking the lead, supported by the media, and upheld by the citizens. Certainly, changes in self-identity from male to female seem strange to many people and certainly ridiculous to others. In some respects, trans issues are similar to racist issues, where society members have to be informed as to what acceptable behaviour is expected to be endorsed by all society members. Within that frame, there has to be laws that punish anyone acting prejudicially against any minority. Often these guidelines have to be written into organisational policies and steered forward, where in just recent years in the UK, black people have purposely been encouraged into being employed in jobs not normally as accessible as it is for white people, for instance, acting in adverts or other televised productions. It was clear before the killing of George Floyd that there were a lot fewer black and Asian faces flashing across our screens than now. UK society needed a push, and organisations made sure they endorsed a fairer, more open, and less prejudiced view. And if for the black Asian community, then so for the trans community. In the workplace, they must be employed with equal opportunity, and in the personal spaces available for women, if any trans people are classified as women, then they have legal rights to those spaces. This fits the logical order of the law and how politicians create boundaries or rearrange them to allow equal access, be they a biological woman or a trans woman.

Self-identity rights were made lawful in 2004, which is a long time ago, and in recent years, the voice of what trans people want and how they should be respected has become louder. They want to be treated as a woman if possessing the biology of a man, or as man if actually a biological woman. Others who are neither men nor women in their own minds (non-binary) want to be treated as that category, even though, in law, non-binary does not exist because according to biology there are only male and female genders based on two sexes. Gender is a word with an ambiguous meaning, it originally meant what sex someone is but it can also mean how someone chooses to portray themselves, or relate to themselves in a type of refection different to what most people would who share their biology. It involves the holding of factors available from two sexes where the distinctions are based upon behaviour, cultural or psychological traits. Generally a non-binary person believes that she / he possesses traits suited to both expressions of the sexes.

Within all the social changes taking place, there has to be inherent logic directing people to make those changes or to accept them, much of which is a wave of activity that is not stipulated to us that we clearly understand it or know about it consciously. As we enter this new Evil Tran era, we must tread precariously. And because we have yet to make this a uniform socially aware shift, some trans people have to endure the burden of what is an awkward social situation whereby the other person assumes them to be their mere biology and not their lawful self-identity. Should they have to endure that? Arguably not, as they have been cleared legally in this context, but socially, it has not caught on, as we generally assume a man is a man and a woman is a woman based on biological signs such as breasts, facial hair, or social norms of dress. This means we are out of synch to social context compared to the law.

Until we have encouraged and reprogrammed this new thought process and applied it to everyday action or experienced it enough in literature or fictional examples like soap dramas, we will continue to address who we see by what we see based on their obvious male or female anatomy. We might make an adjustment based on knowledge that trans people exist but most of the time if a man has a beard and wears trousers, we assume he is a man and wants to be known as a man. If a man wears a dress he probably wants to be known as a woman, unless a cross dresser like Brad Pitt. You won't undermine the anatomy principle at the biological brain mechanism level is my totally confident belief. Habits die hard, especially those formed in societies through thousands of years, mainly in relation to some inherent biological understanding where the brain quickly assembles logic for who might be a suitable partner for sex and, more specifically, for the creation of our species. This format, whether described exactly as I have said, is roughly the rule in biology across the many different species' spectrums.

We are biologically driven in general to fancy another sex or even the same sex in a minority of people or both sexes for some. We cannot stop the automatic brain processes taking place when we find ourselves physically attracted to some people we like the look of. DNA altering and adjusting inside our species, through great amounts of time, maintains this type of instinctive processing in us. It is a part of being human. Self-identity is a modern phenomenon and not really a biological drive at all, but if argued as a biological drive, it is only found in around half a percent of the population. It is a sense that informs the self whereby they feel different from the classical identity of others that we might call common. It is a variation from the normal theme of how to represent the human species and experience the self. It certainly is challenging because, generally, humans bound themselves into accepted groups, surviving in packs that include ways of socially identifying similar traits in one another. The poor old tranny wearing a dress with his hairy muscular legs is a clear sight to stand out and be ridiculed or prejudiced against, just as many people are who simply dress with skirts supposedly too short or so exotic most of us find it strange, odd, or peculiar and would never be seen dressed like that. Muslim women are not often seen in revealing attire; football hooligans have to wear their team's colours and chant prejudicial songs at other team fans. Politicians wear suits and attempt to find a look that is deemed respectable and affable in personality to others. Self-identity understood this way applies to us all, and with a trans person, they are just a bit more driven to look like the other sex in their chosen format to express their personality, or for non-binaries, a feeling of no sex at all or a bit of both.

For this trans reality to fully immerse itself into common society we have to accept we all have ways we like to express including what we choose to dress like and sort of identify ourselves to be. Not all women want to wear a short dress, others would never wear trousers, and some men are never seen in a smart suit while others are never seen in jeans or colourful ties. For some reason we all like to project ourselves with how we feel comfortable.

A trans person has an unlikely need and awareness to project a sense that they are not the same as what their sex is, and from this sense they try to fulfil the needs of that self. Imagine if you were made to dress in a fashion you hate. You would not do it, and that is just dress sense playing out in you. Imagine if your sexual identity were alien to you. You would want to change it, and rightly so is my honest opinion. This is why people stand up for trans people and their rights. However, there are many aspects to rights that people do not understand, and from a position of ignorance or fear of looking anti-trans, people just produce a blanket response and stand with the trans agenda from a point of view that simply does not take into account what human rights mean in certain contexts. This might cost a company an employee and even a financial loss at the courts for unfair dismissal.

In other situations, you probably have no concept of the up-and-coming problems we all face in regards to trans people, human rights, UK law, and how to mentally contextualize a social situation in the correct fashion. If not understood, you will be reacting the wrong way in your social communication because you have not prepared yourself in accordance with the reality set by law and the new social convention that should fit that law; you will be acting illegally.

Currently, actually calling someone Miss who is a Mister is not a break of law, but if it causes them distress, or arguably so, then the police have the power to intervene. This is the natural conclusion of Evil Tran – a logical complex that interrelates to law, social situations, punishment as education, and where people in general just fall into place and live hoping they do not come unstuck or pretty much do not care to worry about the unlikeliness that a trans person would even complain to the police. The point is friend: he / she can complain and make it very clear that the person addressing them has assumed wrongly that he / she is a he when in law he is actually a female and wishes to be known as such. If the law stands as it currently does, then we have to learn this cordial compliance, or some of us will face police arrest. In turn, why should any trans person have to put up with our out-of-date mindsets, especially if it genuinely upsets him? Oh, sorry, I meant if it upsets him or her, they / them, or is non-binary! That's the real modern progressive way to see it. Maybe there will be a condition where, if we make a genuine mistake, we are clear of charges, which, if so, only adds to the difficulties in learning these complex social situations. Generally in law we are not excused by a lack of knowledge pleading ignorance. Be careful of hate speech because often it is not hate whatsoever.

Suddenly, we enter a realm of confusion where we must cultivate intricate understandings in order not to break the law. Fulfilling that law is hard to process because why would your mum or grandmother understand that a transgender person has the right to dress manly while identifying as a woman? It is a principle of law that a person can do so. Suddenly, we as citizens are expected to know and follow these obscure laws and endure lectures from corporate sympathizers representing cancel culture, the media, and so forth. This is a consequence and natural mechanic of Evil Tran. And it has all come about because political and social understanding recognizes the need to accept trans people for who they say they are, even if they are not real women. Which arguably can cause distress, and intervention from the police if you post something to that view on social media. You can voice an opinion, but if it is deemed a design to cause distress and harm to someone, it can be called hate speech. I would just like to say, for the record, that no trans people have been deeply distressed reading this book! If they have been, it was not intended. If it were intended, explain where in this book it was intended and how you know that. At what level of the principles of descriptive language can police legitimately prove or decipher what would cause reasonable levels of distress? Suddenly we are living in a mess only untangled by legal experts and academic styled brains, which means trans-unknowledgeable people are at a social disadvantage and open to punishment and chastisement from university, media, corporate, and political people.

In my rhetoric here in this book, some trans people or their sympathizers might call it hate speech, which is just a ploy to manipulate and challenge anyone who speaks out against people who quite literally do not care about any female member of society. At its core, trans reality is one made around forwarding everything they want, as stipulated by trans organisations and activists. They go on about how these people are the victims and never consider that women and children find it an oppressive experience when some biological male is next to them in the shower room, or that they have to be taught men can be women.

Meanwhile, toilets across the UK have been transformed into unisex spaces, such as hotels, which may not matter for many people, but many women do not like this new anything goes concept. At the gyms, a woman needs to check if a biological male can shower there. And if females play football, maybe a man will join in as a woman. Because this inconvenience is not a daily experience for most people or has not happened to them yet, it is merely a law and social condition that does not make much difference to them until that one day they were not expecting it but encountered it. Few people go to swimming pools or gyms and use the showers anyway. And shared toilets are not the greatest inconvenience for any woman, as she is in a cubicle, as would be the trans person. So we rarely hear of a great emotional response generally within UK society. The people moaning and groaning, like me, seem to be sensitive to the principle of the law forcing women into a corner in a situation when they are either naked or semi-naked. Then there is the intellectual sense being forced down our throats, ordering us that men can be women and that we have to shallow this opinion as fact. It makes people like us feel as if we want to puke, as if some little Nazi guy is going to turn up and order us to behave, watch what we say, or face arrest. This is a social reality where police look at all complaints of hate speech, which is ambiguous much of the time when understood from non-expert eyes.

But the law is the law, and the social reality we find ourselves in is fitting to the law, so if anything we say is technically illegal, then that is that, but trans people use it as a ploy to oppress people from voicing their opinions. What I have written here is fair and balanced and in accord with non-hate speech, although to some sensitive souls, they may cry because I referred to them as men in dresses or used terms with meaning found in the glossary section at the back of the book. But they are men in dresses. They are not biological women, and who defines in our minds if they can ever be women realistically to the standards we set for ourselves? No one. All they did was create a legal fiction, a pseudo woman who no lesbian or heterosexual male wishes to have sex with because, to us, it would make us feel physically sick. This alone shows what we think of the idea that a man can be a woman. You could not imagine a man in a dress is anything like a biological woman for sex. If, in principle, we reject these people for sex, then obviously there is a reason, and that reason is that these women are not the normal type found across the earth; instead, they are a substandard mere psychological entity acting feminine, many with a blasé attitude, while others are timid and nervous to even show themselves as trans women. They certainly are driven to be like women, but we should not feel sorry for people and agree to them being real women if we do not think so.

And again, I ask anyone reading this that if you would not sleep with a trans woman or trans man, then obviously something in your brain and the desire you feel is informing you they are not the same in some way as women or men. If so, why are you accepting them as real women? What an argument based on psychology! Or that biology does not count? In that case, why are we not sleeping with them as if they are real women and men? You don't mind them invading women's spaces, or you feel sorry for their psychological plight, or you don't care to care, which is all fair enough, but either these people are real women or they are not. And if they are not, they must, for many mixed reasons, be defined accurately and sent back to the spaces that belong to them. They can still dress and act as they want, but we won't have to put up with them as some sort of living embodiment of a woman when really they are the embodiment of a social political fraud, a politically correct conundrum played out as virtue, love, and care for the minority species found across the earth who suddenly have more rights than the majority. We have been mugged of our very thought process from which we create values.

Meanwhile, Posie Parker would disagree with me on some points and find it very distressing that I feel sorry for some man-bitch in some circumstances (which is pretty much how Posie sees them and thinks of them as such).

Suddenly, whatever I say here distresses someone in society. But if I do not speak as I find, I distress myself. How some writers circumnavigate the political correct attitudes so that they keep their jobs and are seen as civil and balanced by as large an audience as possible is beyond me here. I would feel sickly inside and would rather have those that can stomach my coarseness on occasion as a minority than appeal to the intellectual mob that I don't much like anyway. Okay, I am exaggerating: I actually feel strong dislike for most academics, albeit they amuse me or are useful for information and intelligent insights, but overall they have too much influence on society, and they have played a significant role in forwarding the trans agenda with their pseudo theories.

One key intelligent point to all I am saying here in this book is to inform you that after twenty years of a passed law, the trans person has the right now to argue that society should not assume all men are men but that some are legal women, and once so, we as a society should adjust our mindset to the new ways. We adjust how we drive to the new laws introduced on the roads and other laws like gay rights, noise pollution, and other factors of law, so why not for trans people?

Understood, please realize it gets more complicated for both sides of the trans argument, where on one side we have people who are anti-trans and their rights and on the other – supporters of trans people and their rights. I find myself at a slight variation of both views. If the law says men can be women, then women they can be as defined by law. If the law says they can shower with my mum or girlfriend, then shower with them they can. If the law says I misgendered someone and can be arrested, then I believe I should be arrested because I know in my heart that every man I meet now could self-identify as a woman, hence I should proceed with caution. But I do not expect this law to be fair to less informed people and tell me where we stand in the following example which is a true story. A guy I know works in a hotel as a porter and he spoke about a 'butch lesbian' who once a week arrives in a van to deliver produce. He tries to accommodate her but is unsure to ever call her dear or luv as he might other women. He always helps her carry stuff and she likes his polite manner. So he asked should he call her mate or pal, and is she a transgender. I told him that just because she is a macho lesbian does not mean he should not call her luv or dear as she is a woman. As a lesbian she probably dislikes transgender men (biological women who identify as men). She would find it terribly insulting if he treated her like a man just because she is lesbian and dresses like a man. But if she were a transgender she might be insulted by being called luv or dear. He asked me how does he know the difference. So I said he does not, so why not ask her name and call her by that. He seemed relieved and laughed at why he had not done so as he has known her for months once a week for minutes at a time. It then occurred to me that the woman may have not been lesbian at all and certainly not transgender. She may have been just a heterosexual woman who dresses appropriately for a van delivery job in jeans and trainers and t shirt and has short cut hair. If my friend asks her is she lesbian or transgender, a heterosexual woman may feel deeply hurt at being thought of as lesbian or transgender just because she dresses as men do. This example shows how we all make assumptions and can easily upset anyone if we apply the wrong way of enquiring. If people will really get arrested for this type of social situation it is quite simply ridiculous and not thought through by the politicians who favour making misgendering someone a criminal offence.

Evil Tran has become a morally draconian, oppressive, and confusing state of affairs for society members given the new position they find themselves in. A position as frightening as having to endure a naked female next to me in the gym showers because she is a legal man. You may not care, but your partner might, and what about if it were your mother or wife next to a man in the showers? My advice to anyone moaning and groaning is shut your mouth and cry, or cop it sweet, take it on the chin – this law was passed in 2004, and trans people have the right to what the law allows them. Your moans and groans amount to hot air unless, on one fine technical point, we call a referendum in relation to whether a biological man can be a woman in a legally agreed sense we as society members agree to, and not just 355 politicians. This is our right to decide important life-changing issues that are of the greatest instinctive importance to us.

In the early days of trans theory and street sense, trans women were 'not real women'; this perception later developed into 'trans women are real women.' The problem here is that they are not real women in the way people recognize women to be. And so this leaves us mentally challenged because suddenly we have to accept men as women while our brains naturally continue to inform us to judge based on physical appearances. That is where we find ourselves in social law reality. If someone has the right to self-identify as the opposite sex why would we ever give up our right to identify them as men based on biological appearances?

We did not grow up being taught men are women who say they are women or ID as women, or that any academic political argument makes them so that we have to adhere to because others know what is best. It is like saying we need specialist knowledge to know the difference between an orange and an apple. You may consider that a human is far more complex than an apple, and my example as a comparison is poor, citing that psychology and biology have to be understood clearly and scientifically. Firstly, it is clearly understood scientifically that men are men and women are women; the majority of experts agree with this. But I will remind you again that we do not need any experts for most things that we identify. An apple is understood as an object identified as the thing we know it to be. If we relied on experts to identify an apple, we would need the advice of biologists and even physicists as we process the intellectual contents of the descriptions that they could produce. In everyday terms, we do not give one toss for such information; we just sensory process objects and use them or avoid them, but we know what they are and what we do not know someone invariably shows us how to use that object. In the case of a woman, we have our own very complex innate descriptions of what she means to us. It is not a complex, difficult thing to address value to. It is a simple thing where never have we said a man is a woman. If anything, we have identified them as sexual, gender, opposites, as a clearly identifiable perspective. A clear meaningful context in the mind men use with apparent appropriateness like we might try to seduce or impress a biological woman based upon a physical attraction. Or help a woman carry heavy objects. We have this right to choose what is a woman or what is a man, based on simple identification methods we use for all objects more or less. It has been established, by us the people over great amounts of time. Meanwhile what has not been established is that any biological or psychological aspects categorically exist that define any biological men as proven women. If the transgender community wishes to present a list of these traits we can be certain most of the trans community fail on their own made up biological definitions where they lower the entry to any male who has grown breasts. Most do not undertake any physical alterations whatsoever. And as for psychological traits, again this preposterous idea would have to list aspects all trans women have matching biological women. Most trans women do not have anything like a similar list of aspects certain to belong just to women.

I do not like the thought that I should be seen as a possible woman, even on technical grounds, because firstly, biologically, I am not a woman, and secondly, no one has proven in the history of self ID that the definition of men and women should exclude biological reality. How dare anyone preclude this entry and boundary to being a man or woman: which alone is entry to the trans-Nazi state – a dictatorship not based around morality to honestly and integrity to intellectual consistency and honour to what has been proven already, but rather the fulfilling of a trend to challenge and alter based on will to argue.

In other words, what we have in the trans community is a minority of people with opinions who believe a woman is not biological by any definition and that a woman is all psychological. If so, men can be women because some men have the emotions, thoughts, and experiences of women. The key weakness of this argument is that women seem to have a unique biological makeup, the result of which allows them to give birth. My call for a referendum holds that fact as a key argument point to suggest that politicians have not upheld their duty of care to the standard we expect when allowing a law to be passed whereby biological men can be given female status as if they were real women. This is quite literally an impossible conclusion for them to have made based on one key objective fact: the outstanding criteria for being a man or a woman is the biological distinction where the male is the sperm bearer and the female is the egg bearer. Who proved such a distinction should be ignored when defining a woman, or any female of any species? Amazingly it has been ignored! But I am unsure if proof played any part in the outcome to the political process. I think a muddle of mixed thoughts prevailed to serve the idea to level up with human rights.

If we all agree to ignore biology as a factual part of a woman, then yes, the law is arguably defined correctly, but if we do not, which obviously we do not, then the law must be changed via a referendum to the meaning that biological men cannot be women in law. From which they lose the rights to toilets and showers, sports, and whatever else is a women's only club. Unless politicians state that men that self ID as women can use women facilities, which is a different argument completely. Here I am arguing that the definition of a woman must be clear and once it includes biology then men cannot be women as defined correctly in law.

Fundamentally, biology states that females and males have been decided based upon their definitions, which simply state that the male produces sperm and the female eggs. How people identify themselves does not alter biological principles. Are we to change the gender classification of all species to what their character is like?

Secondly, humans have always used the sensory information we can see to decide the worthiness of a sexual encounter or partner. We do not look for biological scientific explanations; we identify maleness and femaleness based on historical consistency from viewing all the males and females we met. This includes an understanding that the anatomy of women is dramatically different from that of men. Connected to this biological preference is our fortunate group preference to seek the opposite sex; if not, the human race would hardly exist if most of us were gay. This is how the human race got here – loaded with this biological addiction and fascination for the opposite sex. The sex of someone is a distinction we have an innate ability to identify, and it is a crucial part of our lives. All of these fundamental rules, regulations, ways, and powers we each possess have been undermined by trans-intellectual pseudo-reality, where groups of thinkers and arguers have successfully hoodwinked others in places of power to feel sorry for nutcase men in dresses parading as women to give them women status because if not, society will be seen as perceived, through human rights laws, to be victimizing their social identity.

From this starting point, it was then understood to allow them the female status they desired without much reflection on social impact or what it could mean from a logical, sensory, and intellectual perspective, where there has to be a reflection about the integrity of what sensory information means and how it relates to the category we perceive as being women. Without this understood, we end up implying that biology does not count to help us classify a person, which is a bizarre idea and on par with saying that a car, airplane, television, table, and almost all objects should not be judged based on what they look like to know what their purpose is or what they are.

A male cannot give birth without a female reproduction system, something we must all appreciate and respect in our minds as a fact of life, so basic, a kid understands it as a reliable piece of information that is universally informative, hence maintaining integrity of thought and knowledge. Just because it can be argued that a male can have female psychology and matching expressions, and even a few physical attributes like growing breasts do not make him much of a woman, at most half a woman, and even this argument is tentative.

Politicians should have said men can ID as women, but they are not women based on biology, and they cannot enter any female spaces. This might upset trans people, but so what to that. Should we allow them child status if men say they feel like children? Can they be black or Asian if they are white? Can they be a train driver because they say so? They can be a tranny driver and that's about it.

Just because I say I feel and think I am such a thing does not make me that thing if that thing has physical attributes that I do not possess. If we ignore this as a principle to discern things, we lose clarity and abilities to discern things. We lose knowledge as we open up boundaries that do not fit their appropriate place. It is a recipe for regression, not progression. The brain makes quick-fire distinctions; it does not wish to deliberate complex, targeted arguments to decide what a woman is in a social setting. And if our brains do decide to get involved in a debate about how a woman should be defined scientifically we include biology and powers from that biology that give birth. You might argue we ignore science and instate human rights for individual choice.

What I have written here is not to make friends with trans sympathizers who ignore biological science and ignore the wishes of most people within society. Such people are part of Evil Tran. If you are dumb enough to think a cat can be a dog because the cat thinks it's a dog, I will leave you to the suffering of ignorance to which you belong. Maybe you believe the earth is flat. Maybe your spirit and intellect are flat; you just vegetate towards the likes of the educated mobs from the university system, where many support the idea men are women if men say so, often because they do not wish to be seen as arguably horrible to them. They focus on some ridiculous argument that some men feel like women and that people are more than their biology, which may be true but does not mean we are detached from biology to define us as male or female.

On a personal, one-to-one level, it is not nice to say to someone you are not a woman if they are acting as a woman; we are generally tolerant. However, there is much more to all this than just being tolerant and humane to others; there are bizarre knock-on effects such as losing intellectual clarity and integrity. Suddenly a man is a woman when really few people think that is actually so. And once so, we have to ask why that is and why any minority intellectual explanation should supplant our daily historic rationale. Are we to believe a minority are more intelligent to know what a woman is than us? Further, men can invade all spaces that are personal and protected for women. Most of us find this a disgraceful choice forced upon female society members. Do this minority of thinkers again have super powers that we the majority simply do not have?

If you believe something, does that make it so? Trans-logic states it does make it so. They say they are women, and politics agrees with them.

The question is do citizens of the UK agree? No is the general answer. And once so, we must insist on a referendum or face Evil Tran outcomes, which are challenging society under a mixed bag of arguments that are pushing the boundaries of logic and honesty about what the truth is and forcing us all into a corner where, unless you have absolute proof of your calling, the whole matter of what a man or woman is can be challenged and reinstated.

Because of the law and this social creed, there are violent knock-on effects, which technically you and I have to agree to if men say they are women, like, for instance, showering with your wife at the gym. Let us look at another knock-on effect.

Stonewall is a lesbian and transgender-supporting charity and lobby group. They guide organisations worldwide on how to support the transgender community in the workplace and continually inform organisations that they should allow trans people to use the toilets, showers, and changing rooms of their chosen gender identity. In law, there has to be a specific reason to stop a man who is trans from entering the female shower room, like if he could feel unsafe being prejudiced against, or if there is a reason suggested by any woman using the facility that her dignity, privacy, or safety are threatened. Other than that, he more or less has the right to enter where he wishes, as any given symbol on the doors saying there is a division based upon male and female sex means he can instate the gender identity act in accordance with the Equality Act to clear his presence.

Stonewall also informs the lesbian community about how they should treat trans people.

Evil one: the Stonewall organisation ordered the lesbian community to embrace men who call themselves women as if those men were lesbians.

If lesbians object, Stonewall tells them to 'get over it'.

Have sex with men in dresses as if they are legitimate women or be accused of being transphobic is the Stonewall accusation to the general population. In other words, they told the lesbian community to subvert their sexual preferences for the complete opposite sex because of an ideology! While telling them that transwomen (men in dresses) who want to have sex with lesbians are lesbians themselves. Maybe, in trans fantasyland, but not in hard, stark, biological reality that we all perceive. A lesbian prefers biological women to men for a sexual encounter; if not, she cannot be a lesbian! Technically, according to the definition in law, Stonewall is right 10% of the time, because in law, any man who gains a Gender Recognition Certificate is a legal woman, (only 10% of men achieve this status in law) but I would have thought Stonewall would have had the morals, decency, and honesty to understand that a lesbian falls in love with the normal-bodied female sex, not the gender recognition certificate for a relationship.

If you say this is not evil, then try to have sex or a relationship with someone you wish not to have sex with and see how it feels. It feels like the losing of the soul. Unless, of course, you are a prostitute who sells the body for cash, or an idiot who sells the soul for Stonewall transgender ideology.

Lesbians, for centuries, were afraid to reveal their sexuality because society had a biased ideology that women should not date women or feel deeply attracted to them. Lesbians have suffered the afflictions that weak ideology brings to their sense of individual freedom; they know what oppression is. Suddenly, Stonewall believe in the same sort of oppression.

If you believe in their view or argue it, you are living a lie and embracing a complete distortion of reality. The exact term they unleash on any lesbian for rejecting these ugly retards of intellect is femmephobic. I put it to any man who says he is a woman who subjects any lesbian to an intellectual argument as to why they should have a sexual encounter with him – you are heterosexual, not lesbian, you fancy the opposite sex; if not, why would you consider a lesbian and not another man like yourself who says he is lesbian? Why force yourself upon a biological woman when there are lots of self-identified women like yourself to choose from? And the honest answer is that such men fancy real women; they cannot escape this biological urge and need to impregnate the vagina and not a man's anus.

My word for these men is tranny-retard. The idea is that if they really believe a lesbian would want them, they must be mentally retarded, and I suggest an academic study to find evidence to support the theory that they are actually retarded to some definition on what we might call a 'spectrum'. Literally, a Trans Ideological Spectrum: TIS. By which is meant that the trans reality and structure for evidence is often just a convoluted set of speculations, a little bit of logic here and there joined together like parts of Frankenstein (Frank theory) so that a whole is produced via tentative ideological strands – very well presented, I must add. If not, how did a man walk into a woman's shower rooms unannounced and unnoticed? Only via speculative argument and academic reasoning by the likes of people such as that intellectual slapper Judith Butler, a high-end talk-write-you-to-death for decades self ID fiend; a woman well versed in gobbledygook who can sell and fashion that a woman is made and never born; bring your own professor to aid you in the deciphering of her fancy paragraphs, such as:

'On the contrary, if feminism presupposes that 'women' designates an undesignatable field of differences, one that cannot be totalized or summarized by a descriptive identity category, then the very term becomes a site of permanent openness and resignifiability . . .'

Many say (on behalf of the feminist groups that sided with Judith and embraced trans women as women) that we should agree with her just in case she understands something we cannot decipher from her words.

This makes more appeal in the left-wing lesbian Guardian broadsheet from Judith:

'Perhaps we should think of gender as something that is imposed at birth through sex assignment and all the cultural assumptions that usually go along with that. Yet gender is also what is made along the way. . .'

I could collapse under the weight of such utter bollocks when she further adds, '. . . we can take over the power of assignment and make it into self-assignment, which can include sex reassignment at a legal and medical level'.

Judith even negotiates the claim that our sex is socially constructed, not (as most of us think) biologically given. With further insight, she explains that sex and gender are redundant distinctions to make. She is bound by her own logic about gender as a construct, and here, sex is like an illusion of sorts when normally understood as a distinction from gender. If she knocked on my door to sell me double glazing, she would probably convince me to make a purchase also for my next door neighbour, given that I listen long enough to her, oh sorry I meant: they. In tranny land, they prefer not to be called he or she often enough but choose to select pronouns to announce themselves.

Pronouns attributed to Butler are: they, them and their. (Holy Cow, is Judith a tran-goddess!?) Which basically means how we should refer to the clever woman who is known as one of the greatest intellects of modern times . . . God forbid I misgender the bitch; she would surely unleash a tirade of words so confusing that her intellectual gladiatorial might would leave me even more convinced that I do not agree with her. Me, myself, and I are how I like to be known (they are the three people I only care about with aplomb). But: 'Their, they, them,' Butler the wicked witch has a committed following in third wave feminists movements, which is the style of feminism developed from 1992 onwards, where they would argue to bend 'me myself and I' over their intellectual knee and spank the misogynist (they love that word and can't wait to band it about even though they rarely understand what the word really means in its rightful context) as they bow down to their woman hater exterminator Judith Queen / King of the transgender people (a sort of Trans Moses figure) who set men in dresses free to wander the toilets and showers and all women's spaces because what a woman is, 'fluid' and evolving and changing and who knows at the end of the woman journey they might even turn back to being a man once they have had enough of being a woman. They will if we have a referendum and people vote on what a woman is, and we not be led by 'them' these intellects like dear sweet Judith and that twinkle in 'their' eye that more or less says I did you all up like a trans kipper.

Judith basically says that how we act, supposedly as definitive to being female or male, is learned during social intercourse and not biologically attributed. This makes certain sense in many respects, as boys played football and girls never did, but now worldwide girls play football, talk football, and even box, so who is to say that all we do isn't learned during social interaction . . . such is our gender identity, as we introduce different social variables as we might another language where a few words here and there can become a natural part of our foreign vocabulary, or in this case, our woman's vocabulary. But it has to be said there are no clear list of distinctions, like football for males and netball for girls, as with emotions, feelings, and thinking that clearly categorises women from men.

I am certain many men could learn some of the ways of a woman, like cooking, laying on their backs during sex, wearing make-up and dresses, and becoming more emotional at the sight of sad things. The likes of Judith argue that such a man is turning into a woman just as the foetus turns into a female.

At some point, if enough different social parts are strung together, maybe we can say yes, he has become female in his identity. Does such a person need to be self-aware of such a trend in behaviour and consciously state that he is a woman to actually be this woman that Judith and others say exists? As if trans society imposed it? Probably not. Self ID confirms conscious intent from the individual's awareness as it throws the shackles of social oppression away – a medical state dictate that orders us to accept we are male or female, and that is the biological fact you will carry through life.

All jokes aside or my rude remarks slung at Judith, she creates a logical argument fair and square, and I would not wish to skate over her as if dismissing her when she has rightly been credited with acclaimed intellectual distinction (or, as I would classify her, armed with intellect and extremely dangerous), but at what point in the qualities of a woman do those qualities really make you a self-identified woman? Could I reach those dizzy heights by just wearing a nightdress to bed at night alone? Like Grandma in Little Red Riding Hood. Or do I need at least ten attributes or twenty? Who knows is the honest reply. And once so, who then should dictate this agenda? The elites in politics who have cycled women into the realms of men?

Let us suppose a biological man has more attributes of womanhood in his social gender role and psychology than a biological woman has . . . does that make him more of a woman than a biological woman? Argued Judith's way, the trans way, or the social attributes way, I just suggested, we might say yes. But there are other ways to argue it all, and I believe that a real woman, a true woman, has a distinctive biology different from men that includes the superpower to give birth. No baby, no cigar, is my absolute belief. A woman has gender identity and biological underpinnings. A trans woman has gender identity that could certainly in principle match the amount of social attributes that real women carry if we bother to count them and compare psychological and behavioural traits in a scientific observation, but where is the DNA naturally built womb and power to give birth? Without that, you are an imposter, a pseudo woman – a trans woman. Simple as that. And I believe most members of society would agree more with my stated definition of a woman than with a trans agenda woman who discounts biology or introduces the idea of sex as a captured thing via behaviour or active as a spectrum. Butler would totally disagree with me: 'Politically, securing greater freedoms for women requires that we rethink the category of 'women' to include those new [trans women] possibilities. The historical meaning of gender can change as its norms are re-enacted, refused, or recreated'.

'Recreated' by academics like Butler, using their intellectual arguments to influence politicians to make an intellectual decision. Their fancy concepts do not actually sit too well in the minds of everyday people as seen quite clearly by the fact that most of us date real women not pretend women. Had trans women really been reformulated into the concept of what a woman is at the sensory-tested level, we would have seen a general integration of men dating trans women. But as it is, men hold the view that real women have specific physical characteristics understood as a distinctive value possessed only by women and not men. And so it stands that trans women are not suitable for the job of women as a new partner for men or lesbians. This does not mean that some men do not fancy them in their drag dress or that some trans women are not attractive to the senses of some men; just that, as a general rule, they are rejected by men and lesbians as repulsive imposters. This is all the proof we need as a test too far for the trans community, where trans men (biological women) are not dated by women because they are simply deemed biologically insufficient and not possessing whatever it is women seek from men, some quality only men possess. The quality might be muscles, a penis, or the idea of starting a family with that man. All of these are biological attributes and specific aspects women look for to decide what a man is or what of the man they like that women do not possess. There is no argument around this fact. Get real and accept it, transgender men; you do not have the hallmarks of a real man. Real women will always reject you for the cunt you are. A bullying imposter of truth, a ragbag argument based on human rights but not the ideals of women. The women who say you are real men should sleep with you or explain why, in truth, they do not. How would a normal heterosexual woman date a biological female just because that female says she is a man? It is point blank ludicrous. They would feel physically sick at such an encounter. And Stonewall or anyone forcing the claims of trans rights as an ideology to force lesbians into relationships should be imprisoned for Nazi-like behaviour. It is a modern-day intellectual gassing of the lesbian community based on ideology.

Butler and company, including some feminists, assume rather vulgarly that woman is a subject matter that can be analysed enough times it can then be presented in a new light of logic. Yes this is possible but what a man and woman really are, understood as an everyday historical experience, is a sensory distinction where every adult human recognises the visual difference of men from women especially when naked. From which, naked in a shower room there will be a differing psychological experience and speculative conscious judgement whereby many opposite sex strangers especially if alone showering could feel uncomfortable, embarrassed, sick, intimidated or naturally indecent by the experience of the situation. We react to the sex of a person we cannot visualize and recognize gender identity in a shower room but the gender identity in law gives power to that person to shower with people of the opposite sex.

A convenient term used in trans theory that argues that the sex of a person is contained within a spectrum (see Fausto-Sterling who believes there may be five sexes) where we all possess different variables of biological constituents. Gene activity could have stimulated the release of more testosterone than normal in a female during different stages of body development causing some women to grow hair on the face like a beard or lending a physiological advantage as like what men have causing federations to bar women from female sports.

Genes involved in sexual identity can be found in other places than just the Y for men and the X for women. Generally, on the Y chromosome there is a SRY gene that sends the embryo along the male pathway, but if there is an error and it locates on the X chromosome, the male is said to have XX male syndrome and may have phenotype characteristics typical of the female, such as female genitalia. Men who are born with two X chromosomes and a Y chromosome have high-pitched voices and are said to be more feminine in their expressions than normal men.

Spectrum sex could argue that the levels of hormones vary greatly in some cases or that a person's sex is not simply male or female based solely upon genitals or even definitive hormone qualities, where if women can carry more testosterone than normal, the woman might have more masculine qualities than feminine; if so, why can't such a person be said to be part male? This might be so if held to this logical context, but is a person who is like this, female in the binary sense? Yes is the answer because the judgement of male or female is determined on the fact she produces an egg and not sperm. Naked, we would be certain she is female in the binary sense and probably so in clothes. We could all be fooled once or twice at the basic sensory inspection levels in a social setting, but generally, our perceptual ability is reliable.

Anne Fausto-Sterling would argue that there are more than just the clear-cut binary differences (penis or vagina) that are visually recognised and that people are more complex and open to a mixture of rich differences, making the binary, two-sex status questionable. Society likes to encourage intellectual arguments and be open-minded to theories and fresh knowledge, but at some point in the process, we have to compare and calculate what we deem most likely, probable, and fair as a way to decide what theory makes the most practical sense to uphold. We cannot just assume that casting doubt with fresh speculation undermines what is reliable and accurate. It has to be proven as holding more weight of truth if not everything becomes an, if, but, maybe, reality.

In some way connected to this arm of understanding is the principle of what is termed intersex people; which really means people that are not clearly male or female sex due to chromosome, hormone, or anatomical anomalies. An intersex person (in which one in five thousand people more or less exist) may look like a man but have the internal anatomy of a woman. Trans theory states that maybe there is more to biology than just straight-forward male or female definitions. Certainly trans people are different, and this could be due to biology; if so, there is nothing wrong with searching for those reasons, but finding them or theorizing them does not necessarily mean we have found a new measure to decide male and female.

Intersex examples are not typical of transgender people because trans people generally have a definitive normal biological sex that is easily identified by biological aspects such as genitalia and chromosomes, but because of intersex reality, clear examples of disorders show that complicated outcomes also exist based on DNA signalling displacements and how they orchestrate biological activity that later collectively might produce a male body, but clinging to it is hormonal activity that activates some feminine hormone characteristics. If so, we can argue based on this sort of model of argument that emotions and feelings subjectively held in a person are more typical of what biological women experience because of displacements to hormonal levels or other features biologically displaced or aligned slightly differently than commonly found bodies and their constituents. We can equally say that any of this is merely a deviation or defect found in some men and categorically does not instate them as women. If a man grows breasts, he is not a woman; he is merely a man with breasts.

All we have theorized is that maybe certain biological disorders or complexes cause what we mean by trans people, but this does not then mean, whatsoever, that anything found has proven a man is a woman. If anything, it has merely confirmed that a man is not a woman, unless, of course, you simply lower the bar to define woman and man. The cultural and political bar is so low that all you have to do to change gender according to these theories is claim you feel like a woman or simply identify as such. What are the distinctive qualities you are supposed to have that suddenly make you a woman if you are a man, apart from a claim or wish? Once you realize there are no criteria to determine womanhood found in a man, you have to wonder at the whole trans theory to womanhood as being nothing more than a wish to be accepted as a woman. From which they argue that a woman is created through life and not just biologically determined. The question then becomes: should we accept their wish? Added to this is an intellectual meddling method to act disgruntled and ask us, what do we mean by a woman exactly?

I think for many people, they just feel compassion for trans people and sympathize with them, and from that, allow them what they wish for, like entering showers at gyms, because often most people are not at gyms, in public toilets, on sports teams, and so forth, and so never experience trans inception. What we basically have in trans evolving reality is a passed law in 2004 that says they can be treated as the sex they wish to be identified as. Later, this becomes a set of ideas that trans women have validity that they are real women because biology never counted as to what we meant by woman; it was always psychological depths that counted.

Evil Tran reinforces itself by developing aggressive acts in educational processes, insisting students accept that women were never biological entities and that to say they were is to victimize and act against the human rights of a minority. In their labyrinth of Evil Tran ideology, it has become a way of intellectual life for many students to resist the understanding that we always identified women biologically and should do so now. They seem to think they must follow this educated way being forwarded to them or else face punishment. This is like being educated in Cuba and cueing the youth up on ideas of morality and social justice. But biological reality is based on science, not morality. We, as a society, used that biological reality as a method to value women, like giving birth and having their own attractive anatomies, which men find appropriate for a sexual encounter that leads to the whole of the human race. Evil Tran encourages us all to ignore such values found in women, as it aims to cancel the original meaning and value of women and allow entry to weird men who insist they are women as a replacement value. To think this idea has passed in law and is taught in education systems as if all is correct and should not be questioned and is further supported by a media cancel-culture is remarkable. Who would have thought men in dresses could be so successful as to rewire our minds to believe such hocus-pocus? Do you believe they are to blame or the average person you pass in the street? Please do not assume either, it is the educated classes that introduced and fought this cause of logic and act of will – they are the evil perpetrators.

Trans people sneak around unnoticed most of the time, unless in a shower or toilet. All that is changing for most of them is that the press is becoming more vocal, along with activists and outlandish claims that they are real women, while suddenly the youth are being educated that they are real women because we have no right to question their human right to womanly existence. This is okay to a legal extent, but society should make it clear that these pretend women have neither biological status nor psychological characteristics proving them to be women, and remind us all that neither do they need any.

The reason these details are not laid out clearly is that the youth will soon come to ask why a man can really be said to be a woman based solely on human rights. As if human rights are the be-and-all to deciding reality and holding intellectual status as to what a human is. Is being human just a set of human rights? No. And once so, we have to be clear that human rights should have limited rights in the definition of a human. It should not cancel biology and what value we attribute it.

We have rejected science for human rights arguments in the woman-man-transgender (mix and match) reality and added a bit of doubt here and there in biology and psychology to create scientific credibility. This fooled politicians in 2004 or merely helped them pass the law for the sake of human rights. I suspect educators naturally skate over this sort of clear analysis, argument, and conclusion as a way to forward education. Instead, they offer bits of so-called evidence here and there from the mix and match method presenting the overall principle as a modern, decent, progressive way to behave. What they should be asking the youth is whether the definition of a woman is actually achieved by a man to make him a real woman, and if so, why? Then students might be thinking the whole matter through instead of just being told they have to accept and embrace this sort of political reasoning, which is all it is really, a bunch of fuddy-duddy official administrators telling people how to think and behave, a lame concept for the freedom of individual will and how those wills prefer to evolve as a collective. It might be alright to allow men into women's spaces if society agrees to it, but it is ridiculous to suggest there is a resounding scientific level of proof to show men are literally real women. All there is is a human rights concept to show that in around 40 countries men can identify as women. The vast majority of 197 countries deny this right.

I personally do not care to challenge this self-identity right. I just believe that the definition of a woman, and a man, be kept to a fair and honest scientific standard where it is made clear as a point of biological fact that men are not women. The reason this is important to me is that I truly believe most people maintain a logical standard throughout the world that informs them that men are not women based upon biological differences. Once political society encroaches upon our national right to define a woman it is a step too far, especially as it is also allowing a nation's education, media, corporate and public organisations to indirectly or directly inform citizens that men can actually be women. Once so, we reach a degraded intellectual state reconfigured and socially presented as an enlightened modern intelligent standard where society members believe in cancelling other members of society for arguing against this woke sycophantic fraudulence; a modern day illness. Once society allows Evil Tran to creep in like this it is degrading its level of democracy by overriding the intelligence and opinion of society members against their will and is no longer representing those citizens other than to dictate to them.

I have encapsulated the argument in simplistic terms but for experts it allows for a lot of ifs, buts, maybes, unsolved, unproven theory making. Where the argument stands, if biological muddles occur, men might experience these muddles in a feminine way, and if so, we can argue that although biological men are classically male gender based on traditional chromosome and genitalia identification, we know that disorders may cause changes in levels of femininity. The argument is, who decides how much femininity might make one all or half female? We may also say (which is what trans theorists do say and need to say very often to make their legal case) that defining sex should be done by understanding these muddles. Some biological differences found in intersex examples, and further afield from those examples, could apply to trans people who may have mixed biological differences from normal people, albeit less dramatic than intersex people – is all understood to mean that sex can be classified in a different way from the method that males produce the sperm and females produce the eggs and give birth.

The simple understanding is to realize that only the minority view held in biology embraces these theories. And we must remember that the reclassification of yourself from a man to a woman in the UK does not involve any physical biological standard to impress your doctor with; all you would have to do is offer evidence you are transitioning, which may involve a promise to alter your hormonal levels or show pictures of you wearing a dress. You do not have to take any drugs or show further proof of your intentions; you are now a trans woman; hence, it is all just another loose argument and suggestion in logic to imply that trans people have a genuine, undermined biological profile compared to normal people. This type of biological theory may have been embraced to some extent by the political forces making adjustments to the law so men could be ordained as women. But again, we do not know this for sure, and many politicians who voted probably did not have the faintest understanding as to the relevance of these sorts of objections to the binary system of sex classification. Did they even consider that in terms of the entry points from a man to being a woman that the biology is not that relevant; only psychology is?

If I feel under pressure at the appearance of my body and I wish it were more like a woman's body, then I have gender dysphoria and can be supported into trans-land reality. This is a state of mind. Meanwhile, further afield, I do not need to go to any doctor whatsoever, and I can socially transition and alter my name to a female kind and hold the title Miss or the non-binary title, Mx. So to be a woman, I just say I wish to be a woman, because in the muddled thought processes of politicians listening to any biology or psychology reports, they believe there are official objective criteria that can make a man a woman. Fine, what then exactly?

The political people who made these decisions in 2004 should face a parliamentary inquiry and be held to account and questioned individually which when shown on television would uncover just how ignorant and misplaced their thinking was to set the UK society up with a sex invasion or sex negation scheme where in reality anyone can change their gender identity. All talk of biology is a pseudo out of context relationship to the standard that allows entry to trans change-your-gender status – an act of free will a verbal claim from a person. I hereby declare by the power ordained within the trans community that anyone can become a woman.

The gender recognition certificate will not be given without medical assessment but no trans person needs that certificate to enjoy a visit into the opposite sex spaces and if they technically did need that certificate it is against their human rights that anyone insists they show proof of a certificate. In other words anyone can be a new gender and enter women's spaces. In many respects we could burn the garbage requirements officialdom places at the lives of trans people to get a gender certificate and as a society just accept that some people want to say they are women and let them enter all women's spaces – because in reality that is what we do anyway! It all sounds like a bit of a joke but it is the UK political process in action and it needs a review and it needs a referendum to fairly adjust the matter so that society feels right about itself to alter this process or agree to let it stand. If not there is no democracy in the UK as we are led to believe it exists.

Politicians needed some rationalization to their bow of logic in order to have made these gender changes to society. Whatever it was or is exactly they certainly must think that a woman is characterized by self-identity only. Or that it involves a complex muddled biology that has created a normal male body outward appearance but has an internal jumble more akin to a woman and hence a female in experience. All of this can appear to make sense and seems fair and decent logic, humane and reasonable, so why not let men be known as women as it is not their fault they were born with this biology. But like I say – biology of any specific type is not needed for entry to be a trans person, because no specific standard definition exists that magically proves a trans biological state has been reached. There is no biological state, but suppose it does exist for intersex people who are often argued as being half male half female then let these people choose their biological sex if scientifically it cannot be verified.

In general, this type of condition does not apply to transgender people, anyway. There was a claim circulated that it was 1.7% of the world population, which was later proven to be fake news, but still gets misused as a genuine statistic, as explained fully by ex-professor

Kathleen Stock in her book Material Girls, which explains transgender reality, including the fact that Stock was pressured into resignation by campus students for her honest views on transgender issues. The real figure is 0.018 of the world population, or 1 in 5000 people who have a duel type of sexuality. It is all trans academic salesman fast talk and moral human rights innuendoes that passed this lawful right. It just does not stand up when framed, as I have just explained. We have been hoodwinked, misled, and baffled by convoluted science.

The trans science that did tip a political thought process to make a tranny based decision that biological men are women was never proven, and even if it were that is not a good enough reason to suppose that their definition of a woman should be included as a woman because it is clearly a defaulted biologically inconsistent weaker version of a woman than ours, where really the so called trans woman has a man's body – a sort of hybrid, just a defect of a man because it has a bit of femininity. But where they claim it is a misaligned woman but where we have to mention that the trans woman categorically does not possess the ability to give birth and should in all the logical ways we define truths place the trans brigade biological argument as not defining women at all . . . not even in the slightest; let alone reclassifying how we determine men from women in what is a pseudo claptrap misleading lie that politicians have failed to muster with clarity of thought; because a real woman is clearly all physically sound and correct along with the matching psychology aligned to some range to what we term normal. Meanwhile the male body cannot give birth albeit he might in the rarest of cases have a female hormone profile or a female chromosome or some other abomination complex that is not typical and chartered to produce what we rely upon to make babies and breast feed them. Trans theorists choose to ignore the capability of giving birth as any criteria for their definition of women, instead they allow entry based upon a few nagging differences like hormone levels.

You should not lower boundaries to enlist another category into another category as you end up losing definitive information based on distinctions and indirectly a loss of knowledge which arguably is the base to how we hold truth with integrity as a part of our characters to be balanced, assertive, honest, and plain speaking meaning humans.

The younger generation seems embroiled in subjective fact dissimulation, where conspiracy theories encourage lazy thinking by latching onto a possibility regardless of its unlikelihood and interpreting it as a realistic possibility when it is a mathematical unlikelihood.

In relation to trans arguments that men are women based on identity, it is pretty much far out there in the realms of ridiculous conjecture. The whole basis of this new age transition of men as women as supposedly sound logic totally ignores the physical aspect of what a woman is to bring forward its claims to change how we create reality as men and women as distinct categories.

I cannot believe the human race really believes that a woman can exist as a category that cannot give birth via the womb. This is without doubt a key distinction. I also believe the right to identify a woman or man is a sensory power all humans possess, apart from babies. Biology, plus our sensory right to identify a woman or man as we always have, is how we define women from men. This historical method has been trashed by the political powers, who have not done their job correctly in representing society, and because of this, we need a referendum.

Evil two is allowing men in dresses into the women's showers where your mum, daughter, sister, or lover might visit. Politicians in the UK allowed this order, probably because countries like Sweden, since the mid-seventies, have agreed to it. The very idea of decency and privacy has been lost for women in the UK because of this ruling.

You might believe it is not an act of evil. Good for you. Then what do you want to call it when a woman or child is being forced, against her will in emotional murder to shower naked next to a naked man? It churns the stomach; it forces the brain to endure the ridiculous rationalized oppression from the selfish trans community, which insists on their right to shower where the law allows. These people do not care an iota for women.

Since when did we learn that because someone self-identifies as a woman, he is a woman? A ridiculous insidious concept, which people in the UK did not agree to, nor do we agree to ignore biological parameters and powers like giving birth. Society actually believes the political powers used scientific evidence of some kind to formulate their opinions, foolishly assuming biology as we know of it was catered for, upheld into certifiable factual checks before being rejected. In truth, it was point blank put to the side and left apart to decide the whole matter of self-identity. Had we been asked about this process, we would have refused any agreement that men can be women because instinctively, men are men and women are women based on sensory qualification. Exceptions to the rule exist but walk any street in the world you can spot the women from the men clearly at least 99% of the time.

Once you try to negate the habit of 300 thousand Homo sapient years, you go against the natural mechanism of the brain to afford a daily recognition of who is a woman and who is a man as a distinction. A difference whereby each of us creates specific signals that create feelings and emotions we experience and verifies a sense of existence in that moment. Suddenly, we are to ignore this and replace it with another sense that the man before you could be a woman or that the woman before you could be a man.

You will still make the old-school distinction because if you do not, you might find yourself having sex with a woman who is a man, not realizing a penis is not a vagina, as your mind attaches itself to the theory of a woman as a psychic or psychological entity to be embraced. Because this understanding can never be endorsed as a natural reflex and desire, we have introduced a false woman into existence that, in its fulfilment, is really an idea to annihilate the identity of what a woman is from the awareness of the people. This also means they are trying to annihilate a part of our human existence that uses sensory analysis to define women. Such an idea is a deplorable act of evil and the key hope and outcome to trans ideology that I will call Evil Three.

Chapter 3

Showers with the Other Sex

Do you really think that people in general believe a man can be a woman, that such a man-woman should have the right to shower next to someone of the opposite sex at the local swimming pool, or that a girl at school should have to get changed naked next to a boy who says he feels like a girl? The UK law allows these social norms. The law forces us to accept it. A law made by politicians without any consideration of what UK citizens think.

Since when did politicians have the right to enforce these draconian measures in UK society? Apparently, since the 2004 gender recognition act, when they imposed a law that transfers powers of choice to the transgender community to enter any opposite-sex space, if they so wish, if they identify themselves as best suited to that space.

I believe in the feeling of the self and that to know the self, you need to express yourself honestly and freely, you do not want to be hemmed in, as many transgender people feel or closet gays who cannot come out and show themselves for how they feel. They have historically been stifled or stopped altogether from being what 'they are' as Emma Watson, the film star, might say of them.

However, and quite amazingly, the current mechanics playing out in UK society, especially for elites found in the public gaze, are that they have to be exceptionally careful what they say in case it upsets the transgender community and its followers. These followers (I call the tranny gang) are quick to attack anyone who criticizes the transgender view that men can be women and are so because they say so. These people soon find themselves on the tranny train – a system of virtue signalling whereby its gang members artfully position themselves as custodians of societal norms and values. If anyone does not agree to their values, they will do all they can to punish that person by social banishment mediated through social media, where they uphold a currency of threat attempting to inflict financial losses (creating a boycott of a person, service, or product) especially upon any organisation supporting a normal member of society who voices an opinion outside of their transgender own. They are quite efficient and certainly effective at shutting a lot of people up from speaking their own sense of truth. People succumb to public pressure, otherwise the organisation they work for might not renew their contract.

Elite leaders of society now find themselves oppressed by a new social cult called human rights for minorities, where there is a dominant vocal gang sustained in politics, publishing, the press, television, universities, and many more places to influence the publicly understood guiding principles for UK citizens to follow. This includes accepting men who identify as women as if they were women and not to question this narrative, and to show public displays of discourtesy to anyone daring to say a man is not a woman. We should not be using tact and politeness to this tranny gang but be laughing at these so-called elites and the whole trans-shebang for inflicting upon society an obscene logic that a man in a dress who says he is a woman really is a woman. If you believe that – you are a fool, an intellectual mug who should be ridiculed for the ignorance you carry. And further again, if you believe organisational signs like LBGT (Lesbian Bisexual Gay Transgender) fraudulent signs, then you are naïve. What do these organisations mean by 'we support' such minority communities? So what if they do . . . this is not the 1960's.

Why would anyone not employ a gay person? With a transgender it is very possible many of us would feel awkward around some guy in a dress with a deep voice and a beard working on a building site. Yes, we would be being unfair and prejudicial, but do these virtue-sign flashers employ trans people or just say they support them? Anyone can say we support these people's rights, but if you reflect on your life, do any of us support anyone other than ourselves, friends or family? Do we really need to flash a sign for what is obvious anyway? For a company, it is a modern-day ludicrous virtue signal; a way to keep sweet, a gang of sympathizers who may respond and show solidarity to your product or service. Company members mention to others, yes we have to put LBGT on the website because it's the done thing.

Again, I will ask you – on what basis do you reading this really believe a man who feels like a woman is a woman? And why would that idea override our traditional idea that a woman is someone who can give birth, whereas a man clearly cannot, and where women look identifiable as clearly different from men, especially when naked in bed, in the shower, or when we caress our physical gender sex choice.

Ask transwomen (men in dresses) if they really are as desired by men as real women are. They will tell you that men prefer real women, not pretend women, which is all a transgender person is really – an intellectual argument, a law, a pseudo concept, a pretence, an imitation, a legal fiction. A fraudulent concept when compared to the real deal biological entity that has a vagina and many other attributes that physically cannot be matched by men and which is understood, reflected upon, and intrinsically felt and adhered to as a self-image and confirmation of a unique female self; arguably a superior entity in many ways than men because of the emotional accompaniment. If women really are proven to be softer in nature, personality, and character, they rely also on knowing themselves consistent with their physical bodies. They could not imagine seeing a man's body as part of themselves because it makes no sense to their personal experience. This experience is reliably known and claimed by over 99% of all women worldwide. Meanwhile, the pretend women called transwomen lack proof that they are women at all, by any measure of scientific consistency. They stand naked with a claim without evidence. They could be a bunch of pretenders with a mental disorder, for all we know. Such a view is harsh, and I do not like to mention it. I do not believe they are ill with a mental disorder, but gender dysphoria does fit the description of an ill personality. Most governments discredit transgender people with any credibility as to their feminine or male claims. Personally, I cannot perceive how a modern society could stop anyone from defining themselves as they wish. Who cares if some say they are robots? But to offer female shower access, sports, and other female rights is a step too far without conclusive scientific proof and social recognition that the whole package of rights is agreed upon by members of society.

What a man in a dress, at best, can possess is the ability to show himself as if he were a woman, concentrate his personality to that end, and feel that sense of self grow as he expresses himself as female, which he observes in a cultural context. This is the art of psychological manipulation and presentation, a bit like a conman practices to forward his claims, but we can easily argue that many qualities of emotions and feelings are available to each and every one of us that are not distinctly the property of women or men but for women and men. To differentiate the woman from the man on the actions of thoughts might not be as clear and easy as we think, and even so on emotional tangents.

You cannot list a set of emotions that a woman has that a man does not have or cannot have. It is a question of application and making a choice. So when these tranny tarts say they feel like a woman, I contest that notion as humbug. My logic debunks that myth. I call it – feel free, an ability to design one's own emotional reflective actions via continual reinforcement.

Emotions are there to be accessed and created equally for all men and women, it is a range we can all choose to tap into and express in our own individual way and sense of self. It is laughable that the trans ideology points to the claim that women's emotional access is different and secluded from men and that because they have this access, they must therefore be women. They uphold this by saying they feel like a woman trapped in a man's body, as if women have different emotional ranges and feelings. This is a totally subjective view, and impossible to prove that a man cannot possess the same range of thoughts and emotions as a woman. Feminist groups (especially those who detest men parading as women) argue that men cannot know what it feels like to be a woman. But I disagree and suggest to them that they have not really thought this argument through. They are just assuming a muddled conclusion from the claim by men that simply cannot be true. They assume men do not have the same range of emotions and feelings as women. But maybe often men conceal those emotional ranges. Or they uphold an even weaker supposition questioning how a man can ever know what it feels like to be a woman; this could be a legitimate conclusion, but only if it has been defined exactly what a woman thinks and feels like that a man does not.

The fact that these two concepts have never been objectively proven simply means how the hell does anyone really know that they can argue either of those two ways. It is another pseudo-argument where the tran brigade has indirectly corrupted the thought and reasoning processes of others to argue from a platform of deceit, prejudice, and shallow thinking based on miniscule evidence.

What we should be stating is that men and women can feel, think, and share emotions that match, and if so, the very claim from a man that he feels like a woman is a false argument for woman status in regards to thoughts and feelings because any thoughts or feelings can be shown to belong to any person.

We should not assume women produce some so-called elite separate women's range of feelings, thoughts, and emotions not available to men. But the tranny-men and feminist groups seem to agree that there must be some special cutoff point that women possess that the feminists say the men cannot access and the tranny brigade says they do access. Both schools of thought belong in the intellectual misleading trashcan. They all seem to hold hands and run through the garden of misdirection – a social maze of confusion that breeds assertive, aggressive expressions. All part of Evil Tran.

I cannot believe their claims limiting men and women as if they were distinctly emotionally different, as if women were men's superiors in their show of love to fellow humans, the environment, the arts, and themselves. We could write down the emotional character of a million people and find those characterizations to fit men and women equally, like if a man and woman travel to work in the morning and create thoughts and reflections based upon what they encounter like for instance getting a bus, train, coffee, phone call, text, reading the paper, supplying directions to a stranger and choosing a breakfast. Lists of daily experiences, like this, have matching attributes of emotions, thoughts and feelings accompanying them. They would not be shown to be clearly divided. You might show preferred trends at given moments, but some thoughts and emotions would match when men buy shirts and women buy dresses.

All a man cannot know is what it feels like to be pregnant or to have a period, and a few other experiences, like being sexually impregnated, where particular nerve ends stimulated in the vagina create corresponding feelings only known to women. A man can be fucked up the arse for sex, but he cannot feel as a woman can via the power of her vagina. He cannot know what it feels like to be pregnant or experience the female menopause.

Suppose that you could scientifically prove that men and women are distinctly emotionally different. You would surely have to agree that women have wombs that can give birth and that men do not. And once so, it is clear that women are physically known to be different from men and what abilities they have including birth.

If women do have a specific range of emotions that men do not, this can only be said to have been acquired by having cultivated and selected differently from the choices available than how men did. And suppose some men who say they are transgender do mimic or acquire this specialist range; this does not make them women but simply shows them as having this emotional range of women. But what is certain is that all men clearly lack the physical attributes of women. You surely need both the physical and psychological aspects to be a woman. Without fulfilling both criteria in principle, all you can be is a cheapskate impersonation, fooling the intellectual and academic classes to make pathetic arguments that you are a woman. An argument punched out by trans-friendly academics (often with a paid agenda) where the majority of medical experts throughout the world disagree with the trans theories.

Imagine another scenario where a female lunatic psychopath might actually lack that female emotional range; we would still classify her as a woman. She would not lose that female status because there is no measure of proof declaring exactly what a woman is in a feeling, thought, or emotional sense – only the clear traditional method that we look at the physical attributes to make our gender decision. An insane person might not even identify as a woman, having lost the ability to know – she is still known to be a woman. This has been the way of the world and its logical collective thought process.

So why is it that politics is allowing men with some obvious feminine social expressions access to womanhood as if they were equal to women and their rights? Men do not have the physical qualities that a psychopath or insane woman still possesses, which qualifies her as a woman. So men in dresses can only gain access to what a woman is through some emotional cognitive ability that normal men supposedly do not have; otherwise, we might say they are women who do not identify as women! He's a woman and doesn't know it, ha, ha. The local Labour Party might send you a letter informing you that you have been officially recognized as being a woman, and unless you erase a specific range of emotions, you will be classified as a trans woman and entitled to an earlier retirement compared to a man.

I already suggested that men and women's emotional access is not split apart; they have equal access to those natural abilities that, sadly, a psychopath does not. So if we ignore the physical attributes, what this leaves us with as a method to access womanhood is the mimicking of outward social manifestations like cultural dress sense or some etiquette women generally embrace and men do not. If so, this is a shallow way to define women and an easily accessible entry point to womanhood. I wear a dress, therefore I am a woman.

From traditional social norms like dress wearing we can recognize blindfolded who is likely to be the woman. But a drag queen is no more a woman than a cat is a dog, but is rather a clown mimicking a woman, and so too is the man in the dress – he is not a woman; he is just a naughty, cheeky man in a dress. (Show us your hairy legs, darling, would you like a shave?) If he says he feels and thinks like a woman, he cannot prove his emotional range as a woman as distinctly different from what any man can produce. And he cannot know what it is to be pregnant, or finger himself in vaginal stimulation, or to experience periods. So who decides these barriers or entry points? Judah Butler, the slayer of women? Did anyone clarify the doors of entry and exit? No.

So where is this woman that transgender people and politicians claim? And where are we as a society that we allow a self-identifier the rights of a woman?

Chapter 4

Obey Trans

We are in the intellectual and moral trashcan. A UK political societal muddle where on one side of the opinion scale is a bunch of transgenders, student activists who believe that all minority groups are equal and interlinked as part of a suppressed underclass; hence, they fight the good tranny fight sped on by the USA articulate transsexual classes, arts-celebrity-university clans, and media-frightened – hence media-friendly 'Black Lives Matter' 'white middle classes matter because we support minorities' who have spent most of the other decades ignoring how to help black people in the USA. Save that white corporate USA jive for people who believe it. I do not believe it. They generally talk of inclusivity to keep their company's image profitable. The UK is trying to catch up with this self-image big moral sell.

For students everywhere in the UK – what the USA has as a problem we in the UK have, or so they like to think. If the USA sells burgers, makes people obese, and drops bombs on innocent Iraqis, then so will the UK political forces. The USA cleared the transgender agenda through the Obama administration. President Biden supports the trans cause for equal shower access but has never been known to let the first Lady share changing rooms with transwomen. She would never stomach the indecency of it.

In 2010, the UK Equality Act stated that certain groups with certain free choices, like sexual orientation (what biological sex you like to have sex with) along with age, religion, and race categories, cannot be discriminated against. One category that was protected in this way was gender reassignment, which to some people could appear to mean that someone has their genitals altered to the opposite sex. Most people assume the only method to establish gender as a classification between male and female is decided by what genitals the doctor identifies at birth.

However, there is another understanding of feminine and male gender that is established later in life as a method specific to the psychology of a person and their expected cultural behaviour. Some men feel more comfortable in themselves to act like women, and who am I to question that, my darlings, in the tranny world. If a man can be gay or a woman lesbian, then surely a man can be a woman or a robot, right?

Wrong.

He can identify as a woman not necessarily actually be a woman. Further, it is not quite the same thing to compare to being gay because a man can be gay and a woman can be a lesbian without any doubt or argument for that claim – it cannot be contested. A man cannot be a woman if the definition of a woman were the scientific standard of biology. Men have no way around this barrier because part of it holds that women's biology creates an egg and an ability to give birth. Men produce sperm and impregnate.

However, in law, they do have a way around it. Lucky them, and lucky also the women who identify as men. Non-binary people meanwhile might feel a bit female and male or undecided and so do not identify themselves as male or female. Confused? You won't be by the time I am finished. Before I unconfuse you and transition your knowledge, I will just mention that non-binary and transgender men or transgender women do not exist in law. In law, male and female exist, and a person in some way fits into one of those two categories. In law, you can identify as male or female even if your sex at birth is designated as the opposite type.

You can, if a man, decide to reassign your gender by going to the doctor and explaining that you feel like a woman and are in the process of transitioning, which basically means you are undertaking (or just intending) to alter some physical alterations towards your chosen female identity.

This is arguably a ridiculous condition and unfair request set upon the transgender community, because why the hell should anyone have to alter anything about themselves physically in order to establish they wish to be like a woman, unless, of course, a woman is merely a change in hormone levels, via hormone therapy, or a change in physical appearance to a minimal or maximum degree, or just a possibility held in a promise. This appalling requisite should be abolished on the basis of a lack of logic and contradictory standards. Not all trans people suffer from any need to alter their physical appearance anyway. I am pro-trans in this region of law and order, but don't tell the Cissy Gang; they will lynch me. Ironically, the whole matter is decided on the whims of a promise to undergo some sort of physical change; how any of this stands is quite simply incredulous.

What difference to society if he arrives at the doctor and says I feel like wearing pink knickers, can I be put on the trans' list? I don't want to alter my body. Or he says, he does feel like altering his body. Either way he can enter female shower rooms. Should we agree he has the right enter the female shower rooms? It is some test of logic to suggest yes without one clear scientific criteria being met. Such is the bizarre reasoning of the political classes, exposed here, as standing without one real hard boiled objective fact. The only fact needed to enter the shower rooms of the opposite sex is to say you want to be known as a woman.

Doctors classify transgender people with a medical condition known as gender dysphoria, which apparently is a psychological disorder whereby people feel they have a gender identity misaligned with the normal sex of that gender. In other words, men feel trapped in a woman's body. It is said more or less that the person dislikes or despises all their body, or at least parts and that by altering some of that body aids in the healing of the mental condition and accompanying opinions.

If doctors and politicians understand this psychological parameter as a legitimate claim to womanhood (they colluded more or less to pass the law on this matter) why then commit the heinous request to ask people to change their physical appearance when not all trans people have a dislike of their own bodies and a strong desire to alter that appearance? This is exclusionary, surely? The psychological condition is not always solved via a physical alteration, anyway. Even though many men with the condition seek to look like women they actually never go on to even attempt any bodily changes. So why insist on that physical alteration as a medical principle when it is not then insisted upon to receive the gender recognition certificate? I do not agree that men are women, but I do agree we should be fair to the transgender community and reflect this in procedures that apply to them.

I say this physical requirement from the medical profession or physical mimicking from many in the trans community to look like women is proof that entry to womanhood recognizes the physical aspect of the woman's body as proving womanhood. And that it is not just a matter of feeling like a woman but also of looking like one because the physical aspect is part of being a woman. From which, if you understand that logic, automatically a man cannot be a woman because he will always lack physical credibility. Unless you believe the wearing of dresses makes the woman. Many look like rugby players in a skirt, but don't tell rugby players that they might force them to play rugby with them and not with women which is exactly what they did for the sake of safety for women players. Eighteen stone biological male trannies who play for women's teams are dangerous in tackles for women.

There is not one shred of proof that taking a few hormone pills classifies anyone as a woman, even if they do grow breasts. It might make the trans person feel more aligned and good for them if so, but why hold this stipulation as medical guidance? I am pro-trans rights here as well. This is some immoral display from the UK state toward the minority group we term transgender. I think it is against their human rights in some way, as many trans people believe, through misinterpretation, that they should undergo hormone replacements and other medical inputs to justify their legal transitioning status. And oddly enough (to remind you again) the law does not insist this requirement be fulfilled, only that it might be! This is like saying you will buy a car, and so you receive it, but technically, you can't be forced to pay for it. You just promise to pay and take part in the process agreed upon in principle.

Further again, people who call themselves non-binary are part of the trans umbrella, which we could say basically means anything but a normal female or male person as we traditionally accept and know it.

They term themselves transgender, and us normal, traditional people as cisgender, which means a self-identification aligned to our biological sex, while trans people are defined as not being aligned to their biological sex. Non-binary means that psychologically, the person does not identify as male or female, or believes to be a mix of both, or is so unsure does not know. All of which is a psychological condition not a physical one. There are more non-binary people than men who say they are women, or women who say they are men. Who would have ever expected that? Officially there are around a quarter of a million transgender people, or even double that, according to government sources, and Stonewall who say there could be closer to six hundred thousand.

We might have said it would be far more consistent politically and medically to just insist on a trans person to just admit they feel like the opposite sex and will be transitioning (psychologically) more and more as time passes by. This is much more in keeping with what the supposed entry points are to being a trans person – namely a feeling of belonging to the other sex within one's own mind and an opinion about the self whereby the man believes he is womanly rather than manly or that he wishes to dress and act like a woman. Why the hell would all transgender people feel the need to alter their physical bodies? This is an oppressive, draconian measure that must be changed in relation to a referendum where society decides these issues, not the irresponsible, inadequately defined logic of politicians. Hooray for the men in dresses and the women in suits and ties. See, I ain't so bad my dear tranny bitch. My only beef is that you ain't women and once so belong in the other shower rooms.

The question remains from this confusion of double standards: whether such a peculiar political process should be following the definition of their 2010 law when it states someone reassigning cannot be prejudiced against. What the hell does that mean exactly? I will tell you what it means. It means a bizarre logic (yet again) to instate trans people to what sex space they identify with. So a man can say he wants to use the women's shower rooms, and in law, no one can stop him because he says he feels like a woman and has altered his driving license title from Mr to Miss. Only if the gym or whatever organisation states there is a legitimate reason ('proportionate means of meeting a legitimate aim') to separate the biological sexes can a trans person be asked to go to the biological shower rooms, like if safety is compromised for him or the woman. If the organisation does not have sex rules, then trans people can go where they please.

JK Rowling, Posie Parker, Helen Joyce, Maya Forstater, and Kathleen Stock argue that this risks women being exposed to male sexual predators pretending to be trans women or that they are trans women. They are right to complain, but they are also wrong in the sense that if trans women are women (which I am certain they are not) they should not be restrained, while real women are not restrained from having the right to enter those spaces. You surely cannot discriminate just because of inherent dangers. You surely should not be arguing that trans women are a danger to women per se or that men could be pretending to be trans women to be predatory per se. If you make the law that some men are women, then live with the consequences in relation to human rights. In this way, I am pro-trans rights. If not I end up a hypocrite attacking the trans movement based on a principle that should not apply to them to stop them using the facilities of their lawful choice. What should stop them is that they are not women. Arguments beyond that do not interest me. I just believe in defining women and men as having distinct biology from one and other. From there, what society does with it is for society. I believe in intellectual integrity to be sustained, and not allow a slapdash logical format to intrude our standards of truth and honesty. This intellectual integrity resembles the logic held in society members throughout history to discern obvious physical characteristics that differ from men and women. If we have not managed this reliably and fairly then it would render us complete idiots along the lines of not knowing the difference between a square and a circle. Once you alter this standard of intelligence in relation to the power of observation and corresponding understanding you alter human beings within. Altering people within via political design is a dangerous deal to deliver. If you play it play it fairly and offer proof that is scientific or within a range of how people have always created the standard of what a woman is which does include biology.

Why would politicians think that entry into women's spaces by men is acceptable to common society? Why, because the person feels like a woman? Or because, under some technicality, once someone feels like a woman, we cannot object to them using the showers of their choice? Or is it because they really are women? Make it up as you go along to fit in with human rights and a preposterous idea that to fit in; the UK needs to let self ID merchants into opposite-sex spaces? Why, if the criteria for those spaces were always defined in relation to gender by sex at birth? Suddenly, this traditional method and belief system as a value is overruled by the ability to change that restriction via self-identity, automatically placing all men into female spaces if those men wish it. That is basically what the UK agrees to in law as a new modern method to structure society from. Even if the law does not exactly say that these men are literally women, they are certainly establishing that self ID rules the choices to enter any sex space.

Meanwhile, transwomen like to say they are real women, which upsets a lot of real women and should also upset men because now men are conceivably women as they walk into a pub, club, or shower space. (I am anti-trans rights here.) There is no way to tell just by appearances anymore. All you can do is identify visually what someone's biological sex is. To actually know who the man or woman is, you need to ask the person for confirmation. (I oppose this trans right because I should be allowed to make up my own mind based on sex appearance, but legally, this is how it would stand in a context of mind in regards to the law and social norms; that must develop that understanding.) And that is a confusing issue because if these men do not have a gender recognition certificate, they have not legally changed sex and so cannot be known as a woman in law! Nine out of ten of them do not have a certificate, so have not legally changed sex. But if they identify as trans women, we are supposed to accept this in a social setting and must not discriminate! What a confusing madness! I am so confused that I am not sure if I oppose trans rights or feel sorry for the tranny because he / she probably won't have the knowledge base to know where he legally stands, so I will state that it is a perfect example of why I oppose politicians' rights to choose for us. We need a referendum.

Such confusions and stipulations that need so much detailed knowledge are a master class of undermining society, and this is Evil Tran without any doubt. If not stopped, it will ruin society as we have known it. We are generating a fraudulent sycophantic corporate-voiced morality that virtue signals with a full understanding of the advantages of sounding progressive and all-inclusive.

The UK political media process had no right whatsoever to move the goal posts to our social norms and then far, far, worse, encourage a brain-rewiring social education scheme that, in short, informs students that gender self ID equates to womanhood for men. This overall muddle and process are part of Evil Tran. A despicable, misleading, disorientated philosophy and ideology oppressing common sense found in the common members of society, who now face backlash from the educated classes forcing this upon them. I cannot tell you how deplorable I believe these people to be for the intellectual and moral standard they are determined to set for the UK. If it is not stopped in its tracks, it will be the end of freedom, honesty, and power for the people. In its place will be educated elites who passed through the university system dictating as the Nazi state of Germany once did; what I term intellectual gassing of anyone who does not agree to their social tranny agenda, which is really just a platform to express control and instate intellectual power over non-intellectuals. Like Animal Farm or 1984, the fancy talkers must rule over the less articulate as if their words are the word of God. Obey, or be punished, is their mantra.

May they hang by the neck in the common streets with a bloody conscience dripping from their brains for such a despicable intrusion, which probably amounts to a conspiracy at the spiritual levels to take over the souls of society members penning us in like cattle that our partners and children be forced to take showers with the opposite sex and that eventually we just agree to this intrusion as if we should because they – the educated classes – know what is best.

No brother, sister, tranny, non-binary, or whatever you are out there – you must see it for what it is all becoming – a sham on the spirit and intellect of the human race. Do some of you trans women really believe you are real women and should be in the showers with women? Some do, and many do not believe it is right and decent.

And some of you reading this might say, no, I am wrong to complain. If so, date a woman of the transgender kind if you are a man and caress his penis and chest as if it were a real woman, and tell me this is fair. If it is not fair for you, then why would it be fair for society in general as a rule of law that some men get treated as women and shower next to women?

I did not come to make peace but rather to wage war. I seek not the weak and feeble in Evil Tran, but the strong and resilient to fight them, overpower them, and gain leverage over them so that we force them to our moral way and not the Evil Tran process they are inflicting upon us all. It is not their human rights they are insisting on, but their every wish; they do not have human rights covering their every wish. The battleground must be a UK referendum, as this affords us the right to decide what a woman is. This has never been decided in law with clarity.

We have to vote ourselves about who can go to what shower rooms by the standards of tens of millions of UK people and not 355 politicians. That trans people be allowed to transition based upon their own psychological standards and stop insisting they deform their bodies and natural hormone processes, placing a physical parameter on a mental one. If not, we are agreeing to another infuriating logic and power of utter stupidity whereby politicians and medical bodies insist on physical changes from men that they then agree do not have to be followed in order for those men to get the gender recognition certificate.

Some wishes are human rights in my opinion, but others; like whether they are real women, are open to obvious arguments and are more a wish we accept them as women literally when surely we should not, as we do not believe they are women. How can we be forced to believe they are women? It is our human right to believe what we believe. All a tran has in this context is a wish to literally be thought of as a woman, a wish we reject. Next, we will be told that we have to pretend to all kids that Father Christmas is real if the kid believes it, or worse, that we have to believe it ourselves because the kid believes it! When we meet a trans person, we currently have to treat him like he is a woman, but we do not have to believe he is one.

How is assigning the rule that they are not real women wrong when they are not real women? How is that truth prejudicious against them? Suddenly we live in a world where society is replacing truth with an organized lie that a biological man is a woman via means of self-opinion from a community of peculiar men and a political opinion. How bizarre that law should be created and interpreted in this way, disregarding the biological scientific method and the natural way people think and assume a judgment here. What is the exact science to say a man is a woman other than sensory identification as so? A political process where I can say I feel like a woman and therefore I am?

Suppose politicians are right in some argued way; why would their subjective opinion be greater in logic than the wishes of the subjective opinion of the people? What is the confounding evidence they understand that is so compelling, and once explained to us, why would it really be acceptable to women and girls in school for men and boys to enter their spaces? And how the hell is stopping trans people entering opposite-sex toilets and showers any different from not letting them into rape centres, prisons, and sports? If society is prepared to stop them serving their sentences in female prisons or sporting events then why not all occasions? Where is the consistency? Other than that politicians might side with the most vocal group to rewrite these guidelines such as activists, or the UN, or European rights acts, which is like listening to ten Judas Butlers. As it stands within the Act sporting bodies can prohibit the participation of transgender people 'in order only to secure fair competition or the safety of competitors'.

These organisations do not stand for culture, the free will of individuals, or a democratic process; they stand for rules and regulations bound to a worked-out logic that they insist upon. Many things cannot be worked out in this way; many things have to be agreed to by society members. Basically, you cannot show one clear piece of objective proof why a man is a woman or that the process that changed the law was even right to do so, bar some acceptance of human rights and self-identity rights of a person, which a person had anyway because anyone can say they are a woman and dress like so.

These people could have been afforded protections to be treated equally as all other citizens without giving them legal female status and entry to female spaces. Being treated equally should have held a caveat that it does not apply to naked situations where great emotional stress is placed at the senses of women and girls. Meanwhile rape centres will not allow transwomen to work with rape victims; an argument based upon emotional psychological stress caused to women. Why would we only protect rape victims and not all women and children from emotional stress? Since when was their decency and sense of privilege not intruded upon via these naked encounters? It is simply deplorable decision making and to think some people defend these situations on an argument that these men are real women is not right at all.

The Evil Tran group must be stopped because if not, we as a society find ourselves ruled by a few with an elite academic political opinion that they can choose for all of us because they know what is best, like informing us we cannot visit loved ones dying from COVID in hospitals when we may have said we can just sit ten feet away, which would have been suitable. Elite leaders have no right to choose all decisions hidden as regulations. They keep making regulations based on so-called expert insight, and this alone leaves society members phased out of any input or questioning of those rules. It is an educated oppression of the common people, and it has to be challenged. If not, you and I have to accept that the opposite sex can shower with us or our partners, or that we might be perceived as the opposite sex based upon what the politically educated classes say. You would not allow a surveillance system in the showers, so why would you instinctively feel right about another sex being there? Our instincts and sense of decency suddenly do not matter. We have been trashed.

In law, and also technically forced by the logic held within us to social standards of politeness; it will be deemed inappropriate to enquire if a man is a woman or man or non-binary because to do so is deemed prejudiced as you would never ask that of anyone else and hence is intrusive, oppressive, and insensitive to a transgender woman, who at hospitals it has been argued by the NHS changed guidelines that trans people should not have to hear the words breast feeding, or woman, or she, as trans people are sensitive to hearing such words making them feel distressed and emotionally upset. These are the sorts of guidelines the National Health Service has been endorsing, oppressing the majority of the population with a new type of politically correct language.

The NHS has become a disgrace, oppressing ordinary people and their own workforces. I wish them the storm of repercussions they deserve. Although they intend to go back to using words like breastfeeding instead of chestfeeding to endorse common language and not just pro-sensitive trans language. Regardless of their re-corrections, they have sided insidiously with trans rights, as if every word should cater to suit the trans wish list, which is not a human right whatsoever but has been suggested and passed off as one by Stonewall and other lying, misleading groups given certain occasions, all too often.

Chapter 5

Biology Does Not Count

Decades ago, Evil Tran was a bunch of original thinkers who suggested that a woman was more than her biological underpinnings. The transition away from what women are was introduced at the intellectual level as an academic pursuit. This included hardline, in-depth thinkers who wrote and argued original things that women movements latched onto.

Feminists who are not intellectuals might not bother to read or even understand the complex language used to explain fancy articulated notions around what a woman is or is not. They may just regard simple messages from feminist groups that men manipulate women into specific secondary roles within society and that women must fight against this oppression if they are to find themselves and write themselves into the history books of culture and human life. Burn bras yesterday, today burn books that insist women are not men. Why have girls got to play with dolls and take cooking classes at school? Why can't boys learn to cook and men change a baby's nappy?

There are countless examples of what constitutes a feminine social role, but many actions are only more common (not exclusive) to females than what we see in men. Most people's discernments do not accuse men of being women based upon a selection and collection of feminine roles. In instances where we might, where is this consensus defined as a list we can all apply as a standard and proof? Does one need to engage in twenty clear traits of womanhood or two to qualify as a woman? Who decides on this list of attributes? And how does a man really establish, with any proof whatsoever, that he feels and thinks in a way that is representative of a woman? It is a pseudo-concept; all we can really objectively agree on is that he desires to be a woman. Is it credible that we then alter the general sex norms of society? The trans brigade is adept at leading us to believe their people really have objective credibility around how they think and feel as if women, but examined thoroughly, it is baloney – a load of bollocks, not a load of vagina.

As society shifts its social norms into boundaries of what is acceptable, some of those expressions are shared, and that includes cross-dressing, where the man is not a trans at all but just acting trendy, or he babysits or cooks more than his wife or cries more at the movies. So defining any of this to a specific agreement is off the table; all we have is a generalized trans concept, honed, immaculately delivered, and successfully reflected in its outcomes, like, for instance, whether men can use women's toilets.

Generally, women are what we call feminine in their expressions and experiences. Men are masculine and domineering, until, of course, they come home late for dinner having been out with their mates at the pub, and the woman goes berserk, chasing the husband out the door for taking the piss. Men can soon be seen as less domineering once a woman's angry mood is emotionally expressed. I have certainly seen many women bark orders to their partners and dictate and create choices that the women themselves wished for. So the dominant role is not as clear in many one-on-one situations as compared to what feminists might argue – that the male species is always trying to dictate while being formally oppressive.

Are such roles arguably masculine is my prod to you? If masculine means to dominate and lead, I suggest there are a lot of grey areas in how some feminists define men and their attitudes. I have seen men subside into obedience just to keep their partners happy. And I have seen aggressive emotional outbursts from women that suggest they are clearly the dominant masculine role.

What is generally termed feminine normally belongs to females as to what they learned growing up by copying other females in society. This has less to do with biological sex and more to do with how the mind works to produce social roles for the self, like conformity to dress codes, attitude codes that might involve subservience or greater patience with the man's general personality and character, or general social norms and etiquettes that every society is structured with.

The man lets the woman walk through the door in front of him. He opens the car door for his wife. I have never seen women open the car door for men to get in and then close it. At nightclubs, males ask females to dance, and men walk over and ask if they can buy the woman a drink. Women seem to prefer this norm than to them having to do the asking. On dating app sites, the communication channels might balance the approaches so that it is neither really the man nor the woman who is expected to make the dominant approach, which we might term masculine.

'Us' women are more than just what men think and perceive 'us' to be, was the message and speculation of many theorists. The traditional norms in society for women never included a social role; that they played football or boxed, but today young girls take to these sports as society has extended the parameters of gender roles. Women were once encouraged to be housewives, and not have to work. Today, many women have better-skilled jobs than their male partners. Some husbands stay at home and care for the kids while mums work. Many women can outdrink and outsnort men, drive better, gamble more, play better football than their fat-arsed partners, access porn more frequently, and if they go boxing, fight better. Some men are captured within the traditional subservient feminine role as part of their relationship with women, which is my point. This understood, you might get an idea of what the intellectuals mean by gender roles, masculine and feminine, oppression by the dominant type to dictate the social agenda, forcing the other sex into a subservient role.

In general historical terms, it is understood that men play the dominant role, forcing the closing down of women into a category of designed gender subservience. Once understood, male society dominance could expect backlash, pushback, and challenging rhetoric from the academic feminist community, spurring women on to not conform to ways they feel are unfair, exploiting, or oppressive. They were not allowed to vote, remember.

Once women were redefined, understood, and discussed in gender-identifiable ways, society had the structural platform to consider women as being outside of biological and male-idealized constraints. Interesting fresh speculations generally got forwarded by groups of similar thinkers developing a theme in which there were lots of competing ideas and speculations that later through the decades allowed men in dresses to argue that they too shared those classy, rich, in-depth female qualities and descriptions that were gender identified and not biologically created or confined.

The overall classification of these descriptions and development in feminist understanding was one where sex meant male or female biological underpinnings and gender meant the cultural roles each person chooses or is culturally brainwashed to accept and copy.

Why should I wear trousers all the time if I want to wear a dress? Why should I be called a man all the time when I want to be called a woman? Why? There is no fair, modern, logical counterargument, or objective opinion sustaining that a man cannot act like a woman and be treated like a woman because he wishes it. And once this is understood (which is pretty much basic logic) politicians faced with the human rights issues of trans people; furthered the logical structure to embrace treating men as women from a culturally expansive perspective by letting those men into women's spaces, which in turn reflects, proves, and sustains the logic that society is treating those men as they wish to be treated: as women. We might call this predicament a political trap and a political conclusion. They certainly did not wriggle out of it, and in my opinion, society is paying a massive price that I call Evil Tran.

If the men are not allowed in the women's spaces, then society is not treating them as women and as they wish to be treated. From a gender perspective (which I will remind you is one of understanding a social role from individual choice and not the oppression of the state to choose for you) the political logic in relation to progressive democratic society must have felt in a somewhat catch-22 situation, a place with no way out – because if gender logic has a sound argument and looks correct, then the natural conclusion follows to set the men in dresses free and sustain social freedom, fairness, equality, and human rights, all captured in gender-structured logic. A force to be reckoned with, while the freedom of women as a definition separate from men with their own personal space was not really forwarded and expressed as a modern social political phenomenon but was established within history and assumed as a natural position which men could not invade or alter. It has been altered in the UK in a swift coup de grace without any defence or countermeasure from society, albeit there are a few mumbling moaning feminists out there 20 years too late. The Gender Recognition Act was passed in 2004 and unrolled in 2005 following two judgements in the European Court of Human Rights insisting the UK Government amend the law to give transgender people legal recognition in their acquired gender.

Hence, gender ID over decades of theorizing, has managed to push aside the traditional idea of gender by birth sex, negating that a sanctified male is a boy or a man. Initially, by this traditional method, the state chooses your gender as male or female, and that is the law and the logical outcomes to the personal spaces they can administer through. However, today, the individual can choose, via the self-identification process, between being male or female. You may not like this idea, but it is the law, and in some respects, I feel sorry for trans people who literally have the law and righteousness on their side. Normally, when a law is passed, we all submit our wills to the decision or bend the rule if we can, as when we break speed limits or smoke in non-smoking areas. It is just that, equal to this emotion, I am outraged that political powers are seen to be bullying biological women into having to endure men into their spaces. Yes, dear, we, the political process, have decided men in dresses are women if men say so! Many of those who made the decision were female members of parliament especially from the Labour Party.

So where is the woman we all love and know? Accessed by both? Yes is the UK answer, according to the UK government. I can be a woman if I have been born with a vagina, and I can be a woman if I say I feel like a woman, even if I have a penis. Although, to be exact, I only have to file documents changing my title on my driving license and bank details, and I am technically transitioning, I fit the transgender concept, and off to the women's showers I can go via the courtesy of human rights and arguably some interpretation of law. You and I may not like this law, but once it is passed, trans women (men in dresses) have the right to follow the law and use the female-designated toilets or showers. We more or less have no right to say they cannot go into a female space like a shower room if they are transitioning unless specifically defined in regulations why they cannot; a prison is one such example or a boxing competition. We cannot ask for proof of their transitioning if we do not want them in our shower room, so there are a lot of forced social conditions imposed upon us, but it is fair in the context that if we ourselves are not subjected to brazen enquiries neither should any others be.

Again, we see the Evil Tran state its phenomenal impact and influence, grabbing us, limiting us, and informing us like a new program being uploaded into a social robot. Further, we still have to consider that trans women and non-binary people are a social cult, a trend, and also a very fair and honest way to share information or gossip in cultural styles that the youth experience more than the older, out-of-date lot.

In those mechanics, many will side with trans issues and conflicting debates and opinions that manifest, be they unfair or fair, complicated to unpick, or easily understood and agreed to. On the emotional and intellectual plane, the youth at universities, especially, have a part of their personalities strongly influenced by social issues like trans issues. Those habits and how they then communicate those understandings and reflections are part of their continued existence. This is not easily chucked away because people like me say piss off back to your own shower rooms, you tranny bitch. Mine is a natural cultural expression, and we must understand that it is also theirs. When I regard the issue like this, I am fully supportive of the Evil Tran influence I would not wish students to modify themselves to my intellectual emotional cultural wares. The world changes constantly, for better or worse, and whether the students are right or wrong, they have the right to sustain their personalized communication channels. But I do believe, wholeheartedly, that in any social conflict like this where rules and laws have been dubiously passed without consideration to what everyone may think, we should decide our futures on this matter by referendum and not by a societal implosion where elites in media politics and the arts are frightened to speak openly because they might get cancelled as JK Rowling has been.

Evil Tran carries a harsh, aggressive bullying menace with it and is cornering large spreads of influential people into silent submission. This is a poor precedent to manage and is an indication that, in the UK, we are losing a grip on democracy and freedom of speech. When societies manage to illegally oppress people via state authoritarian tactics, like in China or Iran, that is one thing, but when it is done legally via underhanded tactics, as we are experiencing in the UK cancel culture, I believe that is far worse because people think they are acting fair and square, legal, moral, and just. There is not anything moral in cancelling Maya Forstater and others like her who voice opinions that biological men are not women. To enforce rules like that is a misunderstanding of what human rights are.

Feminist academics are, indirectly, as much to blame as anyone for they argued quite rightly that women were more than their physical bodies or their ability to give birth and cook in the kitchen for family.

Specifically, Geddes and Thompson (1889) (biological determinism) argued that due to the differences in biology of the metabolic state, men are 'energetic' and 'passionate' and women are 'passive, sluggish' and uninterested in political rights! Wait for me in the bedroom, darling, after you have performed your duties in the kitchen seems to be the thought here. Biological determinism invented reasons to justify social and political arrangements favouring men and restraining women. If ever there were reasons to argue against the power of biology, it is rooted here. Or should I say the biological theory of men? Let it spur women on to get drunk with their mates watching women's football at the pub, and return home late well after the takeaway was ordered by their partner. You know how 'sluggish passive' women are, darling, not prone to laddish behaviour as it is biologically impossible! Hence, do not accuse us of flirting with the bartender or looking at his ass we don't have the energy.

Sex, then, is merely biological gender identification as in male or female genitalia, but not all there is to being a woman; which must include how one perceives oneself to be as part of personal identity, choosing how to express oneself through different values and dominant traits of personality and character; gender of the mind, through self-perception and sense of self. Yuk to biology, let us women discard it as the secondary automaton it is trying to imprison us – the unsuitable and unstable ambitions men have for us as proven through history. Kill the ambitions that men have for women . . . is the rightful chant from women.

Bentley and then Hinsie (1945) were the first to distinguish between gender and sex. Simone de Beauvoir (1949) claimed that a woman is not born but rather becomes a woman. Hence, your DNA chromosome bundles do not determine social character and expression but rather are culturally learned.

Gender role was a phrase coined by John Money in 1955. Rubin (1975) said that 'Women are oppressed *as women* and 'by having to *be* women'. Haslanger (1995) said that the associated traits of male and female genders are the 'intended or unintended product of a social practice'. Mikkola (2011) argues that the sex/gender distinction creates a political outcome where feminists (and not ordinary people) wish to do away with sex as a decider of gender and transfer it to the realms of personal opinion. Robert Stoller (1968) says that sex refers to biological traits, while gender is the amount of femininity and masculinity exhibited by a person. Gender identity was introduced by Stroller and Greenson in 1963. It basically means knowing what sex you belong to, according to Stroller, where culturally, the so-called trans people argue that the sex they belong to is either some naturally caused biological imprisonment or is open to choice through the understanding of the self, where this would strongly imply a heavy reliance on subjective opinion and the experience of the self through social role habits that, if forced upon the individual to be masculine, may well make that male feel ill because his internal thoughts and reflections are actually more feminine. The person ultimately gains a specific sexual identity (probably concealed from others in the initial stages) that is later crafted into an understanding called gender identity. From a perspective informing men and women, they may well have natural actions, thoughts, and feelings that simply do not match the male or female role assigned to most of their kind.

The majority of humans are all-embracing of normal social sex norms, but trans individuals are not in agreement whatsoever. Politicians understanding all of this were led to believe that trans people are worthy women or men as dictated by the brain of the individual concerned and not via the oppressive collective prejudices of the normal (social role) group that most of us fit into, where we use biology to decide male and female. Confounding politicians (and certainly pressuring them) was evidence that trans people suffer terrible mental tortures or social evils like getting beaten up for dressing however they choose. A despicable act from an extreme few in general society.

Different feminist ideas and perspectives shared in culture between groups merged until eventually the trans brigade joined the party, using gender identity as the great divide from the meaning of biological sex, where our gender identity was originally housed and found to be: I have a vagina; I am a woman. Careful, warn the feminists, if you have a vagina, according to the beast called man, you are only fit to be a sexual object, cook, clean, be passive, and told you cannot vote in elections.

While the feminists embraced the gender identity narrative, they could overturn historically conceived prejudices about biological determinants that men forwarded as part of their oppressive philosophy to favour themselves above women. I have to wonder if feminist groups overused that spin to attack men, showing women what men can be like as shown through history, but where the man-mad theory of Geddes and Thompson's metabolic state itself, along with other points of reference to biological determinism, did not always match the changing forces actually favouring women. Obviously, it got rejected eventually anyway.

I do not buy into a lot of the criticism sent men's way. We are not predetermined and printed from a cask or mould where our evil characters are stored, ready to oppress and exploit women. If though we were, we might say that today men have resurrected their evil in the form of Evil Tran, a new male fascism, an upgrade of our superior nature and ambition where men can be women because they say so and so the oppression reoccurs from this new male might. Strip bitch and shower next to me and my phallus, whether you like it or not, if not feel dirty and go home without a shower and believe you have betrayed modern society. This is Evil Tran speaking and oppressing. Where people like Judith Butler are a resounding evil agency towards women.

Whether you agree with my use of language or not, I believe it is so, albeit she does not gas people to death, there are scales of evil in my opinion, and she fits in very well with her clever, loose opinions carefully structured academically. I call that we strip her naked and check her genitals, for surely she possesses a penis from which she speaks . . . a spin of logic instead of me stating she is speaking out of her arse, as the saying goes.

Sorry to be so rude and crude towards you, Judith, but I do possess a spiritual theory that classifies your philosophy as part of an evil agency, and I would be willing to stick my cock right in your mouth to shut you up if ever an intellectual cock existed that were equal to the size of your intellectual mouth. I would be happy to debate you live at any brain-dead university campus of your choosing! I like playing away from home. Bring a fresh supply of flower. The angry mob would not vote me as the winner, but I bet general members of society would. Such is my bet to you or any of your ilk – academics. I am without doubt an anti-intellectual in definition that your lot is to blame for more social evils than of any other kind on this earth, bar that called ignorance! Such is the logical place I find myself here; I don't know who to beat up first!

Whatever the truth may be about a woman, feminists never really gauged the significance of the men in dresses coming to join the party as women and what influence this would have upon the rights of women in relation to women spaces, and worse yet, the very definition of what a woman is as a thing separate from men. Not that all feminist groups are the same, just that none of them filed a legal objection in the USA law courts (an amicus brief) defending women only spaces from biological men carrying the rights of women; through the power of their minds, holding the opinion they were female as if carrying a Gucci handbag. Move over, ladies, the men-bitches are coming in . . . to shower next to you naked, as is our phallic right as women. You are women, and we are women. Cop that, sweetie, whether you agree to it or not. We believe in social rape, you never had the intellect to fend us off anyway . . . we have bigger brains and smaller virtues, so it is we choose to dominate again.

Trans won, and that must not be denied them. They got what they wanted – they entered the rights of women as women. Yes, no one on earth really relates to them believing they are real women. Sure, they get treated openly as women by many citizens, but hidden away in the brains of those citizens is the computational power built through aeons. This cannot be overcome by social pretence to be polite, caring, and courteous.

The crazed lunatics in the USA political parties are quite happy via logical analysis to allow men to shower with women and to contend with other merits of logic and standards to be considered in relation to the Equality Act, which, if not existing, white people would still be asking black people to use the other side of the bus to travel by, or arrest gays, and whatever else they did in the USA in the 1960s.

You and I today might say that is wrong and immoral, but without certain legal rules created by politicians, social standards can drag the past with them longer than they should. I might say politicians are lunatics because they voted for men to shower with women, but at least they consider the minority rights of people who identify themselves as women who happen to be men. The problem I have when being as serious as I can be about this matter is that I cannot understand why anyone would think that a biological man is a woman. No human has ever changed sex. So why introduce an idea where it is stated a person can legally change sex on a birth certificate? They could have said that some men can use women facilities regardless of sex or gender arguments as we currently are framing them. Isn't a woman, according to science, a person with the X and X chromosomes and DNA-created vagina with the accompanying ability to give birth? Obviously not according to the USA and UK political spheres that voted in this insidious demented rule whereby pretend women, pseudo women, or maybe you think half women (can stand without any fuss next to women naked in the showers at universities or gyms.) That is to say, psychologically, trans women are arguably women or match the psyche of women; hence, they are half women. It is certainly a half-baked idea, as my nan might say.

A triangle has three sides, and a square has four. If the trans person lacks a biological dimension of womanhood, he cannot be a woman, just as the triangle cannot be a square because of a lack of a distinctive quality that shapes what a square is. This is the key component overlooked by many politicians who favour the rights of people with weird, quirky ways that they see themselves as the opposite sex when they cannot scientifically be the opposite sex. So in order for this fact to be discarded, politicians had to ignore the science of what a woman is, and the socially conceived idea of what a woman is, and lower the threshold to womanhood by accepting that a woman is merely a person who decides in their own mind they are a woman regardless of biology. In other words, we live in a USA, UK reality that is really saying that some people see themselves as women because of their biology and their matching sense of self suited to that biology, while other women born with a man's body see themselves as women in a male biological body. This is sustained by many of the trans people who make female claims, but medically and legally the UK accuse them of having gender dysphoria they don't accuse them of being factually correct. What an amazing fuck-you-logic that is . . . only a bunch of academics could invent it (sounds like a plotline from the Twilight Zone) and only a bunch of lunatic politicians could standardize it and force women to cower frightened in shower rooms for the sake of the Equality Act. Another way to say it, is that in the UK if any man wishes to gain a Gender Recognition Certificate, and gain legal female status, he must have a condition that was previously regarded by most in the medical profession as an illness. Or in todays' woke politically correct language, according to the NHS, 'a mismatch between their biological sex and their gender identity'. Remember this is a language turnaround not a new verifiable fact. No one in the world has proven a mismatch exists between biological sex and gender identity accept in the cases where one in five thousand people hold a set of biological qualities that makes it very difficult to decide if they are more man or woman. They term these people as having DSD's (Disorders of Sexual Development) or 'intersex' where these very unlucky people with Androgen Insensitivity Syndrome look like women in most aspects but have biological abilities of men to produce sperm and have the XY chromosome of men. Another disorder is called Congenital Adrenal Hyperplasia where people have XX chromosomes generally found in women with abilities to make eggs but sadly these people carry a penis looking clitoris. Here we see genuine evidence of biological muddles where the person is very likely misaligned to their gender identity but we must remember that the transgender community more than 99% of the time are not plagued with these disorders. They are like you and me they fit the category of a normal biology. Their only difference is that they possess an unusual claim; where they say they feel as if they belong to the opposite sex. It is their determined claim that defines them as transgender. And whether you like it or not, whether they have any science to back them up or not: they stick to their claim and this unique sense of self identity. I cannot lack respect for them just because of their gumption or oddness of opinion. They stick to their guns and with it entered the women's showers. Finders keepers losers weepers. To the victor the spoils. I am not trashing their win. I am merely stating they have won it not to the rules we in general society would have decided it. Politicians cheated us. It is a fine example of the elite classes issuing orders to the majority of us as if our understanding is actually irregular incorrect and wrong. And that their souls hold the keys to enlightenment, betterment, order, truth and beauty. What they have done carries all those words of their own self-description to how they see themselves. I would literally hang politicians for this repulsive, manufactured, fraudulent implication about their superiority. I can assure you friend it stems from the university system and not a disorder of the brain. Educate monkeys to dance and sing and they soon believe they have rights that other animals do not. They have paraded themselves leading transgender culture around in circles in a westernised zoo – look what we have discovered.

Academic study and rationale has to consider all sides of the square and triangle and then compare them. An intellectual understanding may weigh the two but will carry with it bias that in this case focuses unfairly on human rights as a right to cheat objective chromosome and ovum reality and therefore ignores the everyday sense of what a woman is as having a distinctive biological status, ignored for the sake of not victimizing men who, on the psychological plane, think they are women or would like to be. They artfully say things like – they are forced to feel shackled to sexual convention, based on some spin of evil biological imprisonment. As in most points of view both sides hold fair observations.

However, there comes a point where the intellect has to choose, but politicians' choices are framed in human rights. This clouded their judgement and led them to decide in favour of people with a mental illness called dysphoria, which in turn appeases the United Nations, whereby politicians dramatically decided that if you have this dysphoria condition, you can enter the spaces of another sex because we in society do not wish to upset your cuck-coo mind.

Really, what the political process has engaged in here is that they have been hoodwinked by a catch-tranny situation whereby human rights protecting a person's sex as a thing not to be discriminated against is suddenly including the idea that a person's gender identity (a concept of the mind) perceived as female is also protected, including joining the female sex as if it were the same sex.

Politicians should have said that gender identity is protected in that any individual can perceive themselves as female if they wish it, but this does not qualify them into another bracket of biological sex, or that this should mean other people in society should believe that person to be of the female sex or gender; based upon the logic, that we generally assume, that biology counts to direct the forming of our opinions on gender. They should have instructed society with a clear exact definition. Where is the proof of this gender entry into opposites other than a statement to a claim or wish? If a man wears a dress, is he a woman? No, he can be a woman by saying he is one or merely identifying as one. If ever you meet anyone who says incorrectly trans women are real women ask them on what basis are they real women?

Just because some trans people identify themselves as female and politicians accept this does not literally mean all members of society should agree they are female. This is actually more apparent within the structure of society as we know it than considered not, by which I mean – most people do not believe a self-identifier to be the opposite sex or even a legitimate female by the wildest of imaginations, but we generally do accept the person sees themselves as the opposite gender. You might think you are beautiful, but we might think you are far from that.

What politicians have chosen to do is accept that if you do see yourself as the opposite gender, then you can be magically transported into the legal status of the opposite gender and then, by some quirk of law, arguably be known as a legal woman, which trespasses upon the grounds and range of what a woman is, which includes her biological structure and the experience we all receive from observing those physical structures like a vagina and breasts, which tells people – that is a woman. Humans cannot get away from the understanding that women have breasts and vaginas and can give birth and that this basic sensory method is reliable to inform us who are women, just as three sides inform us of a triangle.

These prejudices, preferences, and distinctions informing us what a woman is are mechanics played out in all minds and programmed into us via habitual repetition over thousands of years, creating informative perception. If a person does not possess these qualifying attributes, like a vagina and breasts, the normal mind rejects any likelihood that you are a woman. And just because most women think they are women does not mean we should think that if men think they are women, they actually are. No, instead, we actually think such men are mentally fucked up or said clinically – suffer from gender dysphoria.

We are not entitled to feel sorry for them just because they feel like a woman or want to be a woman. Especially to the extent we allow access to being a woman, which means entering women's spaces. Since when did anyone prove that chromosomes and biological DNA-decided structures are not part of being a woman? No one proved that at all; instead, all that politicians did – is ignore chromosome facts as a qualification to womanhood. And in turn underplayed a qualification (namely one general aspect all women possess) which is that women generally see themselves as women, especially when looking at themselves naked in the mirror, while trans women do not, but where in this case political credibility is aligned to the perception that men and their self-realisations their hopes and desires to be a woman, feel like a woman, and so could you please let me be a woman. Such is their chant and plea to us.

Oh, go on then, just because you asked us nicely, we now allow you to be a woman because we have the ordained right to decide such a matter. No one has that right; because it involves the alteration of how we all act using our brains to perceive reality in relation to what a woman is. If that cannot be altered in our minds, then what is the point or reason to challenge the basic natural way we humans do this thing called identifying a woman? Or to insist we be totally insulted and forced to concede to political power, like our mind mechanics and understanding do not matter but political views do.

If a man in a dress came to a heterosexual man and hugged him and asked him to have a wild, passionate affair, that man would run away, repulsed at the new legal woman. How many heterosexual women would go on a date with a biological woman who says she is a man? And from this example comes the wisdom and proof that people do not see trans women and trans men as legitimate women or men. I am genuinely sorry that this is the case from the trans perspective, but reality and our likes and preferences within it speak for themselves, and us normal heterosexual men simply do not fancy pretend women called trans women. And with it gay men want real men with erect cocks, not some nutcase woman with a vagina who says I am a man.

I might seem insensitive to the trans community, rude and improper, but said politely if they have gender dysphoria, a mental illness in all likelihood, and I say to that oh so what if some people want to live as a man if a woman, that doesn't make them mentally retarded humans, insane, or even really a nutcase as I have said it . . . it just makes them psychologically different. But that difference cannot mean (whatsoever under any circumstances) we all be expected to rewire our thought feeling processes and understanding as a collective unit and lie to ourselves a man is a woman based on gender identity. We do not lie to ourselves, but the big lie perpetuated is the rationalization from the trans political media corporate collective we have to buy into this social change on grounds of human rights, when really it is an unconscious collective drive to dominate the spirit of people via the force of intellectual argument pseudo-science and other sickly misplaced actions. People decide who is a woman and a man not a science manual or any academic study. Just as each of us decide what an apple is or orange or beer, or maybe a meal that we recognise and select to eat. We decide these things.

We know what is green and what is red when we see them. We know a car, a cup, a tree, and many other things when we see them. Sure, there are examples that beat the general rule, but those rare examples do not cancel the rule. For example, when doctors encounter hermaphrodites (half male and female) this is a person with rare biological complexities. These people hold distinctive biological proof that they have some female qualities and some male where maybe they can produce ovum and sperm, and chromosomes that are male and female as classically known. These cases are extremely rare, whereas normal transgenders do not suffer from the same medical condition. Normal women certainly do not possess such a mix so these trans people are not women in the normal sense we mean it.

Any argument referring to the rarity of duel sex does not displace biological arguments that state there can only be two sexes. The reasons are simple and regard the method of biology that has a classification method where sex, reproductive cells called gametes found in all humans and all other mammals – finds that the males have the smaller sex cells (sperm) while females have the larger cells (eggs) and the females give offspring.

Human identity such as female gender via identifying female sex has nothing to do with our personal conscious reflections and its mechanics. The outcome of biological mechanics is two sexes, which biologists frame as female and male. If the football association deals in football and the medical association deals in medicine and so forth for all categories of science, the arts, and so forth, each organisation claims the ground and definitions for their category; a football definition does not get taken over in its definitions by the arts or medical groups, nor does a self-identity sociological psychological format infringe upon biological classifications. We can safely state using biology that there is absolute proof of male and female genders based on sex classification. This cannot be overridden. Meanwhile there are no biological or psychological definitions of a woman according to the self-identity rule. All there is as a method to decide and prove gender is the claim from a man that they see themselves as female.

The misinformation around the possibilities of more than two biological sexes is a perfect example of the fraudulence in academia, generally relying on the principles of arguing for the sake of any argument available to it or for the sake of prestige or payment elsewhere. Until every country, university department, and biological department in the private sector alters the two-sex distinction, we can all agree that logically there are only two sexes. If not, we would be left with accepting arguments out there on the fringes of possibility where definitions are obscure, misleading, and entering territory that is like the football association telling its swimming counterparts what the rules of swimming races are. Such is the determination and efforts of academics; a minority try to argue against the rules and reasons of the way biology classifies a two-sex human system. We all learn at school that all species, more or less, are male and female. What a bunch of men in dresses think means nothing to a biologist and certainly not to me where I prefer to follow the facts and signposts to those facts. And the fact is my tranny friends is that you have no scientific basis and definement to clarify what you mean by a trans woman. If you were to ever state a needed level of hormones classifies a man as a woman or some other biological aspect you will find it does not apply to nearly all trans women anyway. If you were to apply a set of psychological structures you might do better but alas I cannot find what these parameters are that upheld qualify you even on the psychological framing of logic. There is no genuine access for men to be women other than self-identity composed as a wish to be a woman.

You literally wished yourselves into existence and on that note alone I wish you all well because in some way I find it rather charming than alarming. But at least accept I am right in my definition, I do not pretend trans women are women. This is why all of this is so heated for people, we do not stand against trans rights whatsoever, we stand against the fraudulence in the definition of what a woman is according to some trans people's views, their supporters, and politicians' laws. There is no clear cut understood meaning in law the majority of us agree to because we all believe a woman to have a biological certainty attached to her. That is what we are angry about and arguing over.

Politicians have done society a terrible disfavour, and in order to put this glaring mistake right, we must call for a referendum where the majority of society members can decide once and for all if it is fair to say men are women if they say so, and that if they are not women, surely this means they should not have the right to enter any women's spaces that women have traditionally sanctioned as belonging only to them.

It is possible politicians can argue based on human rights, that if the tranny is not a real woman they are to be allowed in the women's spaces because they identify as women. If so, why? What because those men wish to enter women's spaces? How is that a human rights issue? It is a mere wish list. That is a different argument from gender and sex identities deciding who is a woman. That would be an argument around what trans people are allowed to do because they want to do it. Surely we, as a society defined as a majority, wish to say men cannot enter women-sanctioned places, spaces, ways, and wishes. Why would a minority want, supersede a majority want? We should not pretend and argue falsely, as activists, media, and public and corporate organisations do; that equal rights equate to allowing all people the same rights. In some situations, this principle does not apply whatsoever. A man cannot be a woman unless he qualifies as such. Wanting to be a woman does not qualify him biologically or psychologically. But bizarrely, an agreement in law qualifies him as a woman based on gender identity. Just do not imply that there is a shred of biological or psychological evidence that substantiates or confirms as proof that a man is a woman. There are countless examples where allowing equal rights to others is not suitable for the situation. We don't allow children equal rights to drive aeroplanes because they wish it. And the argument stands that a biological woman has traditional biological protections from biological men, where traditionally gender is understood by that biology. Proof of this in a social setting is that all our ancestors desired an exact gender type, where the same gender is rarely wished for. We frame this distinction as male and female. Heterosexual men seek heterosexual females.

Meanwhile, gender recognition by self-identity is not a biological concept but can be introduced as a new way to decide male and female, and once so, means that a man in law can be a woman. But this alone should not allow for an automatic transference of powers whereby men have the rights of women in all circumstances, and the reason I state this is because the two gender types are based on two different principles. The principle for defining the female was always framed using biological distinctions. To allow a modern-day self-identity female the same rights as the biological counterpart is a misaligned idea for social procedures (in some circumstances, like shower room access) because it does not stop biological males from entering spaces with biological females as normally it would. Why would women lose this instinctive opinion to keep biological men away from seeing them naked? They would not. And once so, they have the right to complain that trans women are biological men. Because trans women are only arguably women based on a wish and human rights argument, not a biological alteration that makes them women.

The original general agreement as a social norm was for the separation of biological males and females based on principles of argument found in a category of logic that developed through time and was reliably connected to physical bodily differences that could be visually detected. This logic confirmed that women believe it is indecent to reveal their nakedness before men, and that they wish for a certain level of biological security where they feel safe and can maintain a level of privacy from biological men. This understanding is instinctive and emotionally structured; it is not simply relearned based on ideology, human rights, or any other intellectual baloney. A woman might seek nakedness in close proximity with a male, generally for a sexual type of encounter, not a public experience of revealing themselves to just any man. With this understood, politicians might have argued better and with consistency to say that two types of women gender now exist, with two types of approaches for how protective powers should be maintained in law. Where one of them is biological law and understanding trans women are not welcome naked in shower rooms or other biological women spaces. The other, self-identity law, understands that trans women can enter female spaces where the physical differences are arguably not relevant to physical separation.

In certain instances, like shower rooms, sports, rape centres and prisons, the two types of woman as gender categories do not match in our understanding because psychologically, humans cannot help but decipher the physical differences as being alarmingly important to them as a way to decide whether they enjoy that situation or not and should proceed with that experience. A woman who has been raped by a man and is situated in a rape centre might be traumatised if the rape counsellor is a transgender-woman-biological-man. Equally, in contact sports, a transgender-woman-biological-man might hurt a biological woman because of their higher levels of power, strength, and agility. These protections were put in place because of biological understanding that informs us that men are different from women and women should be separated from men in these situations. In other words – politicians should have said that there are two sexes in law but that within each sex there is a subset category where, for purposes of the law; biological woman is definitely not the same type of woman as a self-identity one, and once so, we must produce laws that exclusively fit the biological woman in biological circumstances. This defined; would mean that everyone is clear in understanding that, for certain circumstances, there must be distinctions based on biological differences. Interestingly, this observation of mine actually plays out anyway because we are continually adjusting rules in sports or changing room access in gyms to protect biological women from transwomen (biological men) where it is clear that distinctions and prejudices are biologically based. Why should the provider of the service decide these outcomes? And why should real women have to share changing rooms with transwomen when the Equality and Human Rights Commission have already stated that a legitimate aim to [exclude biological men from women spaces] 'could be for reasons of privacy, decency, to prevent trauma or to ensure health and safety'. Some women and children will be traumatised sharing changing rooms with men is my point here or feel unsafe. Authorities are bending the law to favour trans people. In my opinion women must start to call the police and explain that they feel traumatised and unsafe sharing toilets or changing rooms with a biological man. This technicality handcuffs the police to take action to favour real women. If not sue the police for not protecting women in accordance to the guidance from the Human Rights Commission. The consideration of the actuality will cause trauma for some women before even entering the changing rooms at a gym or pool.

What I find frustrating but amusing for me and causes me to laugh at the overall process and literally at the people arguing these issues is that there continues to be an alarmingly high frequency of confusing and misleading arguments that might suit either side of the argument fence that is fighting their corner if they can trick everyone into agreeing with them, but which often leaves weakspots in each of their arguments. This is confusing society. Muddling the thought process in general is arguably dangerous for the standards of education and democracy. We find ourselves in a mess. And one example of this is the following situation: JK Rowling and many women's groups say men can be dangerous to women in spaces like toilets and showers. If we allow men in dresses into women's toilets, showers, and changing rooms, we afford a perfect opportunity for predatory men to pretend they are trans women, who will then enter the changing rooms to expose themselves to women and look at women for sexual gratification. Worse, there will be young girls using those facilities. However, because we have introduced a law that says men can be women, we have no right to act with prejudice towards those women and limit their powers. If we do, we act against their human rights to be treated equally. For me, if you live by the sword, you must die by it. If you invent cars, you get accidents, and if you invent a new woman, you must allow that woman equal rights to the traditional woman; if not, you are a fraud as a society claiming equality. You must accept the risk of danger, is my argument. But if, as a society, we agree that there are two types of women, we might discern that in certain circumstances, two approaches might seem fit, where in biologically naked situations or other matters of decency and privacy, we limit the rights of trans women because we all agree they are not biological women. But to make it all as idiotic as possible and confusing, politicians in the UK (led by the United Nations or European Court of Human Rights) have insinuated (maybe stipulated) that self-identity means womanhood. It certainly means the same rights as women. Okay, fine, but if it does and you believe in equality for all women: then why introduce the caveat that biology counts to disqualify trans women from working in rape centres, or living in prisons? Why allow society to be that prejudiced against trans women

– declining their access? The reply is that they have to take into account the decency, privacy, and protection of women. Okay, fine, but protection from whom? Other women who we call transwomen? Why would their different biology make them dangerous, indecent, and naturally infringe on a sense of decency? But if it does, then are we saying trans women are different from real women? If so, define it in law because we are saying they are different, as the examples in prisons and rape centres prove. I won't take years arguing my case for all I have raised here. Society must realise that these glaringly obvious threats to our freedoms, democracy, and general society standards are based upon a collective attack using fraudulent logic, involving the right of organisations to encourage a power structure cancel-culture that is hell-bent to ride the whims of an all-inclusive morality in all circumstances. A forcing upon us all intent on altering our understanding, to take away our personal meaning and ways of shaping our awareness. Once a political and media system bends and distorts information for its citizens in this way, in the call for changes to alter our meaning of what a woman is – I believe it amounts to evil oppression upon all citizens, something akin to an ancient civilization and the dictators of old. The UK democracy and the people within it are becoming a second-rate outfit and not worthy of the worldwide respect for which we say that the UK represents true and honest democratic virtues.

Let us take a look at people who counter Evil Tran and people that are a part of the Evil Tran mechanism.

Chapter 6

Harry Potter and the Trans Triangle Argument

A drama starring JK Rowling, Maya Forstater, Posie Parker, Helen Joyce, and Kathleen Stock as the evil doers. Burn these cissy bitches on fire and send them back to the out-of-date hell they come from. Supported by that cock, Alex Byrne.

Lisa Nandy, Emma Watson, and Daniel Radcliffe are heroes supporting progressive society in a defence of honour, with a risk to the reputation of common traditional society. Let them duel the witches of trans hate from the land of transphobia so that we can learn from their shining example. With added stars, the Centre for Global Development, the High Courts of Justice, and tranny gang members from the media, public and private organisations, NHS, and the Labour Party, who include publishers, celebrities, universities, corporations, health services, and politicians.

We would like to note that all dialogue is fictitious, apart from where you see 'speech marks' or where Russell speaks, but he is a tranny in disguise, a non-entity anti-tran tran! As seen on the cover of this book and on the bitty bitch arrest list, wanted for ten million pounds that we arrest him / her me myself I and force transitioning practices upon him. Whereby he / she is forced to support men in dresses and women in trousers by agreeing that they can be of the opposite sex and should be voted in as the next king and queen, where the transwoman is the queen and the trans man is the king.

NO TRANSGENDER PEOPLE WERE HURT DURING THIS FILM. We do not support trans rights in every instance because some trans rights are not acceptable to women, men, or children unless you don't mind showering with the opposite sex against your will. We take no legal responsibility for any points of view expressed in this FILM and everyone represented is being represented true to their character.

Once upon a time in a fantasy land called Transphobic Hate Speech BECAUSE MEN CANNOT BE WOMEN, a bunch of magical men and women and a non-entity person went for an open discussion, and this is what they discovered . . .

Maya Forstater: Oh, I don't think men are women.

Centre for Global Development: Yes, they are, and you're sacked. We will not renew your work contract.

JK Rowling: I support Maya Forstater; men cannot be women.

Emma Watson: We live in a fantasy where men can be women and women can be men.

Daniel Radcliffe: I fully support the idea that pretend wizards like myself should be understood and respected for all they are trying to achieve in the entertainment business. It follows due to my elitist, university-educated upbringing that I learned how to fight the false forces of cisgender prejudicial reality that victimize the poor innocent trans people who are fleeing for fear of their womanly status from the evil cissy bitch witches Rowling (who wrote me into existence) and

Posie Parker, the gang leader of all that is hate filled towards the trans community, many of who are my fans and who I love with all my heart.

Russell, the writer: In that case, go out with one you soppy wizard. Get stuck into the reality of the fanny woman (a man who pretends to be a woman but undressed has no fanny) for you to fuck, Daniel. Only a stonker, a willy-wonker, for you to suck. Stick that in your wizard gob and sing hooray for dickie hooray for dickie, darling.

Daniel Radcliffe: 'Teachers taught inclusion and acceptance as a matter of course, without worrying about angry parents kicking up a fuss about how being nice to people goes against their political beliefs. If somebody tried to get us to debate them, we just told them to f*** off instead of engaging in a 300-tweet long back-and-forth'. So why don't you fuck off and leave the trans community alone?

Russell: I'm inclined not to leave people like you alone who are dictating a social agenda that we embrace a lie that men can be women and that if we refuse this indecent logic, we should get cancelled by sycophantic celebrities like yourself who never say anything that isn't in the reflection of how it will appear to your social media following and the next film deal. You are not a fraud, Daniel, but you are a person who stands by principles that defend trans ideology acting against all women in society in that you support the idea that men enter women spaces, including naked shower rooms. Or that Maya Forstater should get sacked for voicing a counter-opinion to yours. What right do you and your gang have to supplant women in all they stand for, for men who say they are women? On what basis are they proven to be women? None. On a shorter note, using your method of how to disagree sucstinctly, I hope you fall off your magic broomstick and intellectually die.

Maya Forstater: I'm innocent in all this . . .

Daniel Radcliffe: Maya Forstater should never have received all that blood money after victimizing the innocent trans community, who only want to live their lives and be free to express themselves as they wish.

Emma Watson: Please don't hurt trans people; they have suffered enough pain and torture.

Posie Parker: Fuck them all. They are a bunch of men in drag, a set of slags with their legs open and a cock under their dresses. They wear no knickers, so little girls on buses get a modern-day look of all that they can be when they grow up if they decide to transition and go all the way and have a cock stuck on, which is possible even 'when pregnant', don't you know? (Please contact Posie Parker for the details of such a deplorable factual account of one trans true story).

Kathleen Stock: I was a professor and was heckled out of the university campus because I too said that men cannot be women. I wrote a book called Material Girls, and now instead of teaching the youth about truth and reality, I argue against ranting trans-rights activists that lie and distort reality better than Harry Potter when they chant that trans women are real women because we say so.

Tranny Gang Chorus: They are women because they feel like women. We are part of the cult of trans. And we seek a transgender leader to rule over us and guide us with her or his wisdom.

BBC Corporation: We fully support trans rights and all they claim, and if anyone does not agree, we will not interview you and give you a fair shake at expressing your views.

NHS: We call 'breast feeding chest feeding' so as not to upset trans-woe-women.

Russell: If you support them fully, then why not introduce us all to a prime-time transwoman to read out the news? I support that as a fair and square honest idea to support the trans community. I do not believe men are women, but I do think we should support the trans community better and with matching evidence to what the media claim by offering them high-profile media jobs in front of cameras. Or the lead part on Doctor Who – Tranny Who.

Just think, Daniel, you can ask to star in a Hollywood film opposite a transwoman. Maybe share a sex scene. Why not take one up the arse if you support them? I just want my trans hater fans to know that I am not joking or trying to curry favour with you all. I am saying it for what it is. If you are truly to be supported, then let film companies or news outlets give you leading roles, not secondary ones.

Trans Lives Matter, as do Black Lives Matter, where we have seen a lot more black and Asian people employed by the advertising agencies to star in televised advertisements or dramas in recent years. So why not trans people? They matter, and I agree with that, so why don't the organisations that say they support them give them leading roles that stand out for us all to notice instead of just chanting the mantra, Trans Lives Matter? Organisations do not really support them is my point other than to virtue signal and make good public relations.

Even if these transwomen are not women, that does not matter one iota because even Posie Parker supports their rights; she even confesses to having trans friends (which I do not). She wishes them well in their human rights to exist, but she does not agree with their opinion that they enter women-only spaces. Like me, she does not believe they are legitimate women. Even Posie might say, why can't they play a woman in a film? Mind you, if she doesn't agree with me, she will have my bollocks cut off for heresy, sanctifying me as a transwoman. Sorry, Posie, I don't want to get hung by the neck at Hyde Park any last Sunday of every month as you and your lesbian crew are there discussing how to ruin the trans party and their plans for world domination. I support the blond bitch from hell; hooray for Posie!

Stonewall: Dear Lesbian community, if you do not allow our transwomen to fuck and suck you, we accuse you of being femmephobic and supporting trans haters. You must accept our women. Trans women are real women; get over it!

Young Lesbian: Oh my gosh . . . a man in a dress asked me for a date, telling me he is a woman. I didn't know what to say, so I simply said I was no longer a lesbian but rather a confused student, not knowing what narrative to follow. I mean, how can I fancy a man? I hate their hairy arses, penises, deep voices, and smelly breath. My activist friends don't understand me. They agree with Stonewall that I must accept men as women and have relations with them.

Kathleen Stock: The trans community is represented by a modern-day toxic ideology supported mainly by activists with an attitude, Middle Class 'White Lives Matter' students at universities who call themselves protestors for the cause of trans rights.

Helen Joyce: 'What campaigners mean by trans rights is gender self-identification: that trans people be treated in every circumstance as the sex they identify with, rather than the sex they actually are. This is not a human right at all. It is a demand that everyone else lose their rights to single-sex spaces, services, and activities'.

JK Rowling: 'This has never been about trans rights. This is about women's rights, and activists demand to dismantle those rights'. 'I have nothing but profound sympathy for trans women who have experienced male violence. I want trans people to be safe. I just don't want women and girls to be any less safe'.

Russell: I could not agree less, JK. You are fighting for a secondary argument that indirectly implies that it is okay for women to share spaces with transwomen if the women are not at risk like in a women's only book club. You deal with this unintentionally with others by sustaining a vocal around dangerous areas but not safe areas. The issue here is whether they are men or women, not the dangers of men. Plus, you are insinuating that men are dangerous to women, as if a breed of drunken cowboys were roaming. Most men in most cultures behave like absolute gentlemen towards women. You and the rest of the Cissy Bitch Gang are being far too prevalent, drawing our attention to the secondary argument about safety for women. I believe we should be focusing on the fraudulent claim that a man can be a woman. The danger here, my dear, is the political and academic classes and their refined combination of actions that have allowed men into women's spaces since 2004, during which you, me, and the Cissy Gang said nothing about this issue. Hence our silence supported this issue, which is the prevalent problem today in mainstream society. Not enough people care, and so you dramatize the soundbite about danger. I do not buy into it, even if it is valid, because being valid does not explain and re-examine why politicians have passed this dubious immoral law passed over as a virtuous one, as if we should feel sorry for trans people and as if it is actually morally and intellectually correct. Let us listen to Lisa from Labour, the northern belle, with a hearty voice.

Lisa Nandy: Trans women belong in prisons, rape centres and all sports.

Russell: No, they don't.

JK Rowling: How can you disagree with Lisa and me when we are both saying opposing things? Make sense, or get thrown out of Tranny Hogwarts.

Russell: They do not belong in any woman's space because trans women are not women but rather biological men. So why are people like you arguing a side-line issue whereby it seems to me you are fighting extra hard for women in sport in rape centres and prisons as if they are more important than the majority of women outside of those spaces. They are not more important, and if vulnerable, unlucky for them, but that does not mean trans women are the blame for the potential assaults, but rather ordinary men parading as if trans women.

The point is that if this society claims that trans women are real women, then why should they be treated differently from any woman because they have a different biology? Different biological genders have been discounted by politicians as a barrier to womanhood. Instead, it has been ignored and access gained simply by self-identifying. In other words, the logic of the law is that men in dresses are women. Well, if so, why should anyone care to stop those pretend women only in sports and prisons? We should be arguing for the majority, and the main principle here is that men cannot be women and, once so, must return to their own spaces; as Maya says, sex matters. But for me, I can say prisons and sports do not matter, as if to be protected from pretend women more than all female spaces. The other thing to remember is that those crimes that would occur against women would not be by real trans people in the main anyway but simply by male predators that are not real trans people.

Maya Forstater: I was a tax expert; now I'm a sex expert.

Russell: You mean an academic prostitute? How much did they pay you?

Maya Forstater: No, I am not a two-bit academic prostitute selling my intellectual might to the fraudulent trans cause via the publication of pseudo-science. I believe **sex matters,** as my organisation is called. I try to galvanise women to fight against trans rights to enter women's spaces. Why do you not support our argument, Russell, that letting men who are trans into the women's toilets and showers is dangerous?

Russell: If UK society has been that stupid and weak to let men be legal women since 2004, then we have to embrace those women and give them rights as other women, even if it increases the dangers for women. Just as we embrace cigarettes, alcohol, and cars that kill people, we don't ban those things for the sake of safety. I believe in the main argument that men cannot be women because, as you so rightly say, sex matters as a consideration in determining who is male or female.

We need a referendum to decide if men can be women, not continued lobbying by what is a minority action, which then means people in general do not realise the significance of this issue: trans women are categorically not women, and politicians have acted totally inappropriately. We need you, Maya, Posie, JK, Helen, and Kathleen, to fight for the referendum, as only the people of the UK can put this right, and once we do so, we can go across the water and fight for the rights of USA citizens to a referendum and send all men in dresses back to the pisshole they came from. I am with you all, but don't imagine I must agree to argue like you. I am not some middle-class drone from the university campus. I quite literally do not give a fuck for your etiquette to use preferred pronouns as a matter of courtesy and politeness. Fuck that political correctness crap. Get a referendum or die in the intellectual arguing bin – a painstakingly lost cause, especially when the Labour Party gets into leadership and starts having us arrested for misgendering. It is becoming a Nazi state where people cannot say what they believe for fear of the corporate gas chamber cancelling people like yourself. I blame academics more than I blame trans people for the creation of a monster – a world where ordinary people have to be led and fed what we can do and not do by paid academic expert opinion, like during COVID, when we were told we could not visit loved ones dying in hospitals. We could have visited them. It is their argument structures that led to this debacle – you are a man and I am a woman, if academics say so.

Maya Forstater: You look familiar.

Russell: Yes, you spoke at Hyde Park late October before the Posie Parker gang, and afterwards I said to you – Well done. And you smiled warmly but were called away, and the five women with you did not seem too friendly at the look of a man near you. It will be a lost cause, bar a referendum, Maya. This matter is really about understanding that People Matter. If we cannot choose who is a woman in principle, we have all been robbed of our rights. We have all been raped by trans lie rhetoric mobs that chant trans women are real women. They are not real women. They are moral rapists.

People know they are not real, but not enough people understand the significance that our right to define a woman has been stolen from us via a long-running intellectual and academic mandate to keep laying out laws, stipulations, and guidelines imprisoning ordinary people to those mandates. It has become an intellectual order. Why the hell should anyone have to learn so many specialist terms as if taking a tax exam in order to live life? Once it all becomes specialist, ordinary people cannot join the narrative and debate, and look how the politicians sided with academic thought processes and sold what Woman is to men as once men sold slaves to the USA.

We have become chained to the rules of the university breed, and all they write in company rules that attacked you and sacked you. And then that first judge sided against you not understanding the principles of law himself when he said your views were '. . . not worthy of respect in a democratic society'. How dare he say that . . . a deplorable comment that only goes to show how some people are actually framing acceptable behaviour and respect. He is accepting that if educated politicians have made men into women, we must all accept their brazen logic. Such is the horrid prejudice.

You had to fight onwards until the High Courts rectified the matter and the unfair original judgment. Well done, Maya, my dear, for such a fighting spirit. What a woman you are.

Courts of Justice: Everyone has the right to an opinion, and that includes Maya Forstater when she said men cannot be women. No employer has the right to hold that opinion against someone and sack them or cancel a contract unless that opinion is like supporting 'Nazism or totalitarianism'.

Russell: Isn't it Nazi-like to sack someone or insist an employee shut their mouth from speaking the truth that a biological man cannot be a woman? Aren't people like Daniel Radcliffe and Emma Watson proxies for this modern-day intellectual Nazism?

Maya Forstater: 'Gender-critical beliefs and gender identity beliefs are both protected under the Equality Act, and so, too, is lack of belief. No one can be forced to profess a belief that they do not hold, like trans women are women, trans men are men, and [be] punished if they refuse'.

Alex Byrne: 'Why introduce the terminology of gender when sex is already doing a fine job'. People like Daniel Radcliffe and Emma Watson seem to think otherwise. They are insisting gender identity is akin to the Susan Stryker reflection that; a man and woman become what they are via a complex process of socialization. Hence, if the man enters the traditionally understood female role, then he is a woman via that process. Women to these people are mere social constructs and not biologically related constructs. However, the concept of what we call a man or woman has always been biologically decided.

Russell: We might argue, Alex, that if the two conceptual methods to define men and women are to continue side by side, then we clearly have men-men understood in the minds of people like us, by which I mean I am born with male biology and I perceive myself as male gender in what I am as socially constructed. Meanwhile, a tranny can view gender as a coupled process where being born male but acting female equates to man-woman as a gender coupling. As for Daniel Radcliffe, shall we look at what he says to defend the trans cult? He would have been the sort of student who would have encouraged your demise at the university campus where you were a professor. But as I like to say, Alex, once a professor, always a professor – in other words, always a danger – in that you are always intellectually dangerous and ready to swipe out like any paid intellectual assassin. It is your ilk as much as any that have used their might to support this tranny gang and legitimize their cause to invade women's spaces. It is your mob I carry the hangman's noose for more than any.

Lisa Nandy: 'I genuinely think when I look at the way the debate is conducted, the way that so much of this is based on fear and creating fear about a group of people who are having a very, very tough time'. 'When we look at the way we reduce the debate to things like bodily parts, I think when we look back in history, we will be utterly ashamed of ourselves'.

Russell: Lisa, if you and the rest of the females on the planet do not regard the bodies of men as important in the calculation of choosing a partner called a man, then why aren't women dating trans men? Further to that, what right have a few hundred politicians, or you, got to tell society how to define a woman? The discussion also relates to scientifically understood chromosomes, which are different from men to women. As are sperm different to egg (ovum). Most men look for a woman who can give them children. That power and ability are those of a woman, not a man. Further, there is no validation that acting and feeling like a woman makes you a woman until you can prove that a woman does not have a physical aspect or relationship to reality.

All objects that can be sensed with the eyes have a physical reality that cannot be ignored, and this includes women. You have zero right and zero proof to argue that any woman is not confined to and connected specifically to the body. Especially when we have distinguished males and females scientifically, into bodily clarified, reliable aspects. You seek to cancel that physical aspect in order to suggest a woman is all psychological and zero physical. A preposterous idea. Added to that, there is no proof that women feel or have an emotional range specific to them. That range of emotions is easily accessed by any man and only proves men and women can share that range if the individual chooses to cultivate that range. Hence, there is no proof whatsoever of any uniqueness to how a woman feels, apart from during periods, giving birth, menopause, hysterectomy, and that sort of thing that totally excludes biological males. People like you have totally ruined freedom and common sense, which are based on the integrity of basic knowledge. Academic arguments have been passed through into politics, where yet again the educated classes exploit and dictate to the general public that you understand what a woman is better than them. How conceited is that? How dare you talk about 'ashamed' in some condescending fashion. You are shooting the wrong logic unless you can prove that we have no right to respect and relate to the physical nature of things to aid us in defining things. Objects are recognised by physical appearance not description. All species are identified as male and female based on traditional standards of scientific biology. If we are to alter the frame of how we define men and women, then that is a socially constructed choice for the whole country to make and should be conducted via a referendum where we hear the views and meanings of both sides in the argument. Most people will laugh at you, Lisa, and quite rightly so. People would never agree to your definition of a woman because we all identify women by the same method, and I will bet you and all the Labour Party if I tested you all with pictures of men and women. Your brain scan activity will show a matching method involving physical identification of basic anatomy where it is clear you are defining a man or a woman. Your brain will not reject the notion that when you see a man, he is not a man because you cannot rewire the genetic brain functions we developed as Homo sapiens. You are an idiot to speak as you speak, but on technical grounds, if men can be women in law, then yes, they belong in all spaces, and on that argument, I agree with you. But in truth, these men you call women are not women. And you know it. I would love to test you on a lie detector machine and ask: do you really believe that men are women based on psychological parameters? I will not involve myself in the cheap-shot second-rate arguments about women's safety. It is deplorable that society has allowed this debacle of logic (a man can be a woman) that actually stands against everyone's reasoning processes. That is the real danger, Lisa, and it is so illogical and unfair to normal people if something is not done about it; ordinary people would have literally been reclassified by a modern substandard of logic, intellect, and virtue that endorses a bullying scheme and lies to oppress all members of society, and in turn, your party wishes to send people to jail for misgendering people. Once so, that classifies you as an absolute elitist-asshole, a title well-fitting to you and others that, in many respects, is a title more suited to you than that called woman. You betrayed woman, and if I had my way, you would go to prison for intellectual fraud.

Daniel Radcliffe: 'We have all now realised that racism, feminism, homosexuality – and any other identity – are matters of basic human compassion and shouldn't be the subject of 'debate' because the debate itself is so dehumanising to begin with'.

JK Rowling: I was having a debate on social media, stating a belief based on science that men cannot become biological women. I did not expect to get cancelled from you and Emma Watson for voicing an open and valid opinion. Nor compare my opinion with the theme that I would ever question the rights of gay people, trans people, or black people. How dare you make such an irregular point of misleading logic to paint my opinion that I question anyone's human rights, Daniel. You will cast no spell over my thinking. I invented you, and I may as well end you for the fraud you are. Self-identity has nothing to do with homosexuality whatsoever in the context of truth and real meaning here, Daniel. If I am gay, I am gay, simple as that. But if you say you are gay and you are not gay, then you are a liar or fool, and so too with a man who says he is a biological woman; he is a liar or a fool to support such a false notion.

No one needs to be fed any basic human compassion, as if we need to feel sorry for such a person, you idiot, why would we feel any different for a gay person than our own sexuality – both are as natural as each other. Next, you dead wizard, identifying as gay is not the same category of logic as identifying as a trans person. They are not even similar. A trans person can be gay, heterosexual, or bisexual. Don't muddle sexual orientation with gender identity as if the same category of a problem; they are completely different areas as a problem, where you are suggesting that people who debate the category of logic that a man cannot be a woman are dehumanizing trans people, when all we are doing is debunking a myth, a lie, a deceit in intellectual and academic logic from a minority, whereby we make it clear that: biological men cannot be biological women; such a voice is the voice of truth, not a dehumanising wizard's stick to beat trans people with. We do not wish to live to an understanding that people like you are perpetuating via a method of argument to suggest trans rights, includes that we should agree they are women when clearly we do not agree. It is a matter of collective majority understanding, held as a human right that evolved through time reliably and efficiently. No one has the right to identify with a religion and insist we all enlist in its beliefs as part of our own understanding. We are all perfectly aware and would argue for trans people to have the right to self-identify, but that does not mean we should then, in turn, not be vocal and state the obvious that they should never ever be classified as women, literally or even legally. At least you know there is a difference between legal and literal, Daniel, just as there is between a wizard and a witch. One has a penis; one has a vagina! How they dress does not make them much more than a fashion statement, my dear. It is you and your irrational kind that dehumanise us by stating that we cannot uphold a valid opinion. Your soundbite is a vicious, misleading conceptual context – the sort of falsity that climate deniers use to muddle truth via misappropriated contexts to deceive people. You believe your words because you have not thought them through . . . you have linked the gay, bisexual, and lesbian themes with the trans theme that if understood clearly – we are not saying that trans people cannot identify as women, we are saying they are not women they are transwomen; people with a distinct male biology that once being held disqualifies them from being women, unless you can prove biology does not count to what women are which you cannot. Please go to the anti-tranny wizard's school for a list of what specialist words mean and how they fit categories to aid your education. Or go to the glossary; you might learn something there.

Daniel Radcliffe: 'A lot of anti-trans arguments fall flat when you replace those buzzwords with people who are just trying to live their lives'.

JK Rowling: I was just trying to live my life, but today anyone who voices the opinion that trans women are not real women and qualifies it with scientific references is deemed anti-trans. This is simply not true because, to be anti-trans, one would have to wish to deny their rights to live freely with their opinion they are women. They can live freely with that opinion, but I can live equally freely and say they are not real women because they are not real women. Real women have a particular biology different from men as agreed through time. That is not bullying trans people, as if I were saying a gay person cannot be gay or that a trans person cannot identify as if a woman. You want us all to say they are real women, when they lack the biology of women, well if so, go and date a trans woman, Daniel. Why would you not date a trans woman? And the answer is that they are not women. They would take out their penis and ask to impregnate you. You would disqualify them from womanhood due to their biology. Or are you suggesting that there are two types of woman – one with a male biology and one with a female biology? And your resounding evidence for that is what? An opinion from some men they wish to identify as women. So far, you and Emma Watson have never been seen in a relationship with a transgender person, nor have you asked to cast opposite them in a film, kissing them as a lover. You seem to refrain from that loyalty, but meanwhile, expect all women to be loyal to your rhetoric and allow men with penises naked in the shower next to women with vaginas. Would you let your own girlfriend shower naked at the gym next to a man? Ask your mum how she feels about that. If your mum said she does not believe it is right she should have to share the gym shower with a biological man, and meanwhile a trans woman says he does think it is right – then who is right? You say you support trans rights, well if so are you saying that the trans person is right and your mother is wrong or that she no longer has rights to her opinion? A trans person says he is a woman. We say he is not a woman. Who is right? On what basis is he a woman? He makes a claim. He becomes a woman in law based solely upon a wish to identify as a woman. He does not become a biological woman based on biology. This is a human rights argument and a fulfilled possibility given him in UK law based on some notion of human decency. Meanwhile what most members of society mean by woman is that they have biology of a woman. Once a human lacks that female biology they lack social confirmation to that gender. They only have political confirmation and that relies on a gender certificate which 90% of trans women do not possess. They are disqualified from being a woman. Self-identity does not overpower the biological distinction we use to decipher who is the woman. Who proved that biology does not count? No one. You wish us to move our opinions based on all lack of proof. I have never heard anything so conceited.

Daniel Radcliffe: 'Transgender women are women. Any statement to the contrary erases the identity and dignity of transgender people and goes against all advice given by professional health care associations'.

Helen Joyce: Interesting that you refer to professional healthcare associations. Since when could any of them refute the science that no human has ever changed its sex? How can we erase the identity or dignity of anyone when we agree that a man can self-identify if the law says so? No one can deny this truth available in UK society. What they cannot be is what they are not . . . just as a dog cannot be a cat, so too a man cannot be a woman, a wizard, or a witch.

Russell: Sorry, Daniel, but the judge at the High Court told Maya Forstater that we all have the right to free opinion, even if it is upsetting to others. To deny this right, this social norm, is to deny the very existence of freedom for everyone. Daniel, do you not share equal compassion for women who now find themselves as no different as a biological class to some men via political law. Thought through as relevant in law, we might even argue that men and women today are all the same unless they identify themselves with a chosen gender; only then do they become a difference. Meanwhile, biological science states that a man cannot have a baby and has a different chromosome structure than a woman. You wish that we ignore the science and the way we actually identify men and women using the eyes and brain to decipher them as such? This is reality, but you seem hell-bent with Emma Watson to argue that black is white and white is black, that a circle is a square, or that you and your gang are more right and better at being moral than our gang. This war is about values and what we stand for. We stand for men and women in that we say men cannot be women because of the biological differences. Women cannot be men. If men can be women, please prove that biology does not count towards being human. You lower the standard and magical power of what a woman is by saying any man can be a woman if he says he is. Some value that, my wizard friend?

END OF FILM ONE

Chapter 7

How to Stop Cancel Culture

Here, I suggest a method and intention to stop Evil Tran in its tracks. If I use the term we, it is in the polite hope that you reading this are in my gang. If you are a transgender person, please understand that this is not just about what you want but what UK society wants.

Hit List

We should construct hit lists. Whoever is on the hit list, we then attack financially, morally, and socially for representing cancel culture where they support the ruining of people who voice the opinion that biological men cannot be biological women.

Like, for instance, Lisa Nandy MP from the Labour Party and Emma Watson, the film star. I accuse both of supporting an insidious, noxious movement where men, who call themselves women, and their supporters have literally lied, exaggerated, and confused their way to a position of social influence that believes in ruining people's lives for not agreeing with them.

Any public criticism about trans people or their supporters is called out as transphobic, exclusionary, and against human rights; when really the criticism is simply in conflict with trans-clan ideology to be politically correct towards them, or, said differently, to agree with them or when you don't agree, don't say anything.

Emma Watson, the film star from Harry Potter, is perfect for the hit list. She criticized JK Rowling, the author, for helping to cancel her. Emma posted, 'trans women are who they say they are.'

Celebrities, like Emma Watson, who claim trans women are who they say they are, should be publicly hung by the intellectual neck and ridiculed for what they are on social media, with campaigns held against them for any contracts they currently have. This sort of logic voiced as a virtue is the carrying force, like a strong wind, capturing others to follow.

Emma represents Prada, the fashion designer for women. But Emma does not represent women; she chooses some men over all women. She insults women by upholding that men in dresses are women. Emma forgets that women actually are who they say they are – humans with a vagina that gave birth to the human race. She protects trans people because they are a minority as does the next false prophet of logic, Lisa Nandy, an influential MP in the Labour Party.

Lisa said in a Radio 4 interview, 'trans women are women.' She and Watson have an opinion that they voice, unlike many elites from our side, who are quiet, timid, and frightened to speak out. But Nandy and Watson, like countless others, are factually incorrect on many counts. So let me recap some hard facts and arguments again for you.

First, a biological man cannot be a biological woman. In order for Lisa Nandy and the Labour Party to be correct, biology would have to be discounted in how we define a woman. In law and science, it has not been discounted.

Second, people like Emma and Lisa are guilty of assuming that all men who say they are women are women based on subjective observation of those men. This is trans-mantra logic. But just because they say they feel like women does not make them biological women. And biology counts unless the law says it does not count, which it has not stated.

If anyone is going to support men in their claim to womanhood, then at least know why exactly you do so. Is it because men say they are women, or is it because they possess a Gender Recognition Certificate that lawfully says they are female? Maybe it is both, but often it is absolutely neither when it comes to elites in the public eye. I am not even sure if elites know what sustains their opinion other than what seems to them to be in vogue and a sensible choice to avoid trouble from activists.

Supporting trans people is no different from any other human; they have human rights, but this does not mean we support murderers in their murder; we merely support their rights to be treated fairly within the bounds of human rights, but we do not agree to release them from prison just because they voice an opinion within human rights to be released. We have the right to refuse them, and we also have the right to refuse men from being accepted as real women. We should reject false claims that just because you feel like a woman, you are a woman. If not, we lose our integrity as truthful, honest people. We enter a myth and falsify the truth. We enter a fantasy where the values we normally use to decide between a woman and a man are trashed.

If the law says they are women because they identify as so, then the law and society norms must make it clear they are not biological women but merely self-identifiers classified **as if** women. This is a crucial difference from the continuing confused arguments undermining society's elites, who are attacked and cancelled and frightened to speak up in case they lose their jobs.

Third, please understand that there is no magic bullet under any form of action from any man that transforms him into a woman. At the very best in law, on appearances and socially, he is merely acting **as if** a woman, as far as most societies in the world determine it.

Yes, trans people have the right to say they are real women, but everyone else has the right to say they are not real women. So no one is breaking the rules of human rights to voice an opinion. All are within the moral guidelines and stipulations, and further to this, all are within the bounds of UK law. So why sack people or cancel contracts because employees question the transgender opinion that they are real women?

Fourth, these elites are supporting all trans people. They say things like, 'We support trans women's rights.' In total, there are around 260 thousand trans people in the UK, according to government sources. The Stonewall organisation says there could be 600,000.

Amazingly, only five thousand men have a legally binding Gender Recognition Certificate confirming them as female. But note that another aspect of the law allows all transgenders to enjoy the same freedoms as those with a gender certificate. The consequences are obscene, with women having to shower with naked strange men at gyms or universities, or allow them into their women groups.

The massive majority are legally male but claim to be female. As such, how can Lisa and Emma and organisations that sack people even claim the trans movement is what they say they are? All fail in biology, and most fail in law by lacking a Gender Recognition Certificate. It is the law and politicians that allowed this idea that men can be female. People in society never got to vote on the matter. It was all just suddenly cleared without any discussion with UK society.

Fifth, the gender certificate legally creates a female in accordance with what is called legal fiction, not biological fact. It is a clerical alteration in the law that is a convenience and use for trans people. They can change their birth certificate to the female sex, But I will remind you again that they are mostly male in law, not female.

According to the law and human rights, the trans community must not be victimized by being forced to go into their own biological sex space. They have a right to go where they legally identify themselves to go – the women's space. And women, meanwhile, have no rights to impede those rights; they have to take the shocks of the indecency of biological men showering near them. This is what the Labour Party supports.

Sixth, just because a female gender certificate allows the person to change their legal status, this does not automatically mean they are women, because to be known as a woman, society would have to agree that biology no longer counts. To suggest that biology does not count in classifying someone seems incredible, considering the biology of living things has two sexes classified as male or female.

Frauds

They claim to protect women, but Lisa Nandy and many of the Labour Party politically attack women's groups they term trans-exclusionist hate groups. But really, these groups are just women who reject the idea that biological men can be biological women. Why would they include biological men as biological women on the basis of being inclusionary when men are not women? They are entitled to exclude men under the threat of a social bullying scheme.

Women's groups have the right to state that sex (female gender) counts in defining what a woman is. If you believe this is correct, then why allow men in women's spaces? Please give one reason.

Insidious advice to lesbians and small children

Stonewall is a prime support group for the lesbian and trans communities. They offer despicable advice to the lesbian community and also to small children.

The Stonewall slogan is 'trans women are women; get over it', from which they produce the jump of logic – that any lesbian not accepting one of their men in dresses is displaying femmephobia, which is a ridiculous and misleading term introducing the idea that women who desire women for a relationship have a phobia against trans women, signalling that this is unnatural, when really it is about as natural as you can get.

Stonewall is the key influencer who instructed the NHS to stop using words like woman so as not to upset some in the trans community. They made a video telling small boys to play with dolls and ignore their parents if they tried to discourage them. These are the sorts of organisations that Emma Watson, Lisa Nandy, and the Labour Party support. They are clones of arrogant, selfish people pervading UK society who wrongly believe we have to support a minority and everything that minority wishes for. We support equality for minorities, but not that they should get to choose what toilets and showers they can use.

Biological sex has always been the criteria to decide a woman from a man, so why would a minority dictate to the whole of UK society to do otherwise? Their common trans-misleading narrative is that they are being victimized if they are not allowed to use the toilets and showers of their choice. But really, it is females of all ages who are being victimized.

We must not forget that all males are subjected to this tranny invasion by women who call themselves men. I do not wish to shower next to the trans men's netball team with their tits and vaginas flashing, and I bet a woman would not wish her husband to shower with naked women.

People who support this selfish trans narrative are a threat to UK society. They assume that trans opinions should be automatically given to them because they demand them and that not to give it to them is victimizing them. Hence, they are given entry to women's spaces. This is an illogical request to ask of society because we always identify the differences between men and women via biological differences, not personal thoughts and feelings.

You could say that societies' thoughts and feelings held collectively have always maintained a distinction between biological women's bodies and those of biological men, where women have vaginas and men do not. Why has that supposedly changed in us? It has not. But we are being subjected to it because politicians are today supporting the minority viewpoint, whereas historically they represented the majority viewpoint.

The trans community has challenged mainstream society into submission around these issues. What has followed since is a continued social and legal attack on anyone who voices the opinion that these men in drag are real women. Mainstream people are being closed down, and so-called leaders are generally not speaking their minds, so they keep their media jobs, political standing, and the social impression of being fair-minded to minorities. If we continue in this direction, society will lose its culture and ability to produce free speech.

An exaggerated and misleading statement from Lloyd's Bank

Lloyds Bank issued a public statement, late 2023, regarding the UK Prime Minister, stating that they were 'appalled to hear the rhetoric coming from the Conservative Party conference targeting the trans and non-binary communities. Hearing language that fuels hate and division is shocking . . .'

The Prime Minister Rishie Sunak had said, 'We shouldn't be bullied into believing that people can be any sex they want to be'.

The Prime Minister was using factual speech that biologists agree with: that sex cannot be altered to its opposite. Some people are idiotic enough to believe biology can alter from male to female. Currently, there is a cultural phenomenon where trans-gang culture attempts to force all opposing views held by people into submission by argument and bullying people across a wide spectrum of society, from universities, media, politics, workforces, and celebrities. This involves highly critical verbal attacks on social media and face-to-face threats.

Companies like Lloyd's are publicly signalling that the right to free speech in this context is hatred and victimizing people when really the Prime Minister is supporting the women of the UK who have lost their rights to womanhood to a bunch of men in dresses. Where people are being galvanized to attack and destroy the fabric of free speech and free will to build society as the majority of people choose it to be.

I hope Lloyds Bank investors and customers consider moving funds from their bank and writing to the head office defending women's rights, saying that a man cannot be a woman. Ask the bank why they call a factual statement from our Prime Minister an intention of hate towards the trans community.

Attack

Because of their arrogantly displayed moral attitude and their heavy-handed tactics to cancel people, I recommend group action whereby a system of attack can be reproduced all around the UK upon anyone who defends trans rights to be called real women, as if this were a fact already decided in biology, psychology, sociology, philosophy, and all society members. This trans type of junk collective statementing doesn't pass a 1% likelihood threshold that they are right in their conclusions to say they are real women, given we judge it from them producing any majority of thought from any of those four specialist academic groups. In other words, they are a minority opinion-based, multifaceted group moving like a gang in synchronisation across the social fabric, reinforcing one another and feeling righteous about it. The danger here for the anti-transgender group / real women group, is that many do not feel good within themselves because many are often stifled into silence or compromising agreements that we have to respect trans people at every quarter. This condition could not be more serious to a person, in my opinion, as it is like an emotional intellectual cancer inside eating away at the free will of a person and should not be underestimated just how debilitating this is.

We do not and will not accept men as real women, which then means they do not have any logical right to enter women's spaces. The whole matter whacks of an indecent intellectual standard where the Evil Tran group acts as if morally and intellectually superior; amazingly, this could not be further from the truth, and in many respects, if mainstream culture ever gets a feel for this oppression, we can expect gross toxic reactions. As it is this is a minority pursuit fuelled by social media and public media outlets. People have other distractions, but I commend both sides for fighting for their cause, as at least we show an opinion albeit bitterly divided. I am especially thankful to Maya Forstater, JK Rowling, Posie Parker, Kathleen Stock and Helen Joyce.

This is merely a human rights argument cleared into UK law, nothing more than that. If people do not sustain an attack system similar to how the cancel mob have a mechanism of attack, then they will cancel us socially, and we will diminish in numbers and power. Without a counter mechanism or the same mechanism they use, we will not win. Our power base will subside, the trans culture will manipulate further, expand, and finally enforce their warped sense of reality into people's minds that some men really are women, and that will be the end of that. The victorious, it is said, write history; in this case, they also write standards of logic, social norms, and styles of morality.

Some of us must set up groups that inform people **not to vote Labour** unless, of course, you do not mind a society that forces people of the opposite sex together in showers and toilets and that your husband could be classified as a woman or you as a man. Would your partner be okay with you showering with the opposite sex? Are you ready to go to prison for breaking a Labour Party-planned misgendering law?

Go buy yourself a dress, boys, it might come in handy later when, to fit in socially, you cross dress to show loyalty to your mates at the pub or the Labour Party conference. Me and Lisa Nandy MP can share a shower afterwards at the hotel gym.

Ask Prada to terminate Emma Watson's contract for being anti-women. Post Emma messages, making it clear how you feel. Ask her if she would date a trans man (a biological woman). Or let her mum and nan share a shower at the gym with a man who says he is a woman. Ask the same of Lisa Nandy. And ask all MPs if they support women's rights by defining a woman as being biological and the scientific opinion that women can give birth and men cannot.

Organisations claim all-inclusive policies, and people like Emma and Lisa claim they support the trans community as if in every instance this is the right thing to do, but it is not right to support aspects of the law that lead to infringements and offenses against public decency for women. Society has to be sensitive to women's needs, not just to men who say they are women.

Technically, men can now enter women's spaces for all legal purposes as if they were women in law. But also within the law, women have the right to complain to the service provider, be it a gym, swimming pool, club, etc., and say they feel their privacy and decency have been intruded upon. This means the man has to leave the space. If not, this should lead to a call to the police and a court case against the service provider if you can fund the matter via CrowdJustice which is the essential next step and the only route women can take if they are to get these sorts of personal spaces returned to them.

Meanwhile, UK society must become aware that the law has gone too far. We now need a scientific definition of a woman set in law that is biologically based, from which it is made clear in law that the self-identifiers are not women or whatever they say they are, because this is scientifically impossible.

If UK society does not grasp its right to define women and men biologically, then we face a storm of changes that are profoundly disturbing, where education, health, media, privately run corporations, and more are educating people how to use language without the use of words: she, he, woman, girl, boy, and more. These changes are offensive to the majority of people in the UK because they direct and order all people to be socially engineered by altering habitual language, the very baseline of social norms, by informing them what language they should use or must use. This control mechanism allows educated people to create a way of life in the UK that is formal and logical and set standards around reflections to seem virtuous to the minority calling themselves transgender people. They are literally hung up on officialdom and new social orders via a threat advice mechanism that sacks people and forces changes on people using their services. They have no right to do this as a collective unless we, the majority, allow it.

You and your family may not have yet experienced a direct encroachment from these forces, but you will eventually, and when you do, you will be socially corrected with an air of distain set upon you if you are not seen to conform. This may involve an official warning from some organisation or even a visit from the police to inform you that your words fit hate speech or a type of prejudice that is illegal.

If you do not begin to counterattack this USA-style moral dictatorship, all of us will find ourselves forced to accept changes that we did not choose naturally and fairly through social evolution.

Shout out

We need people to pump out messages via email and social media to cancel culture organisations and celebrities demanding they accept biological women as the only real women – those who give birth to every human on the planet – and to stop this sycophantic USA-style corporate morality that wants to be liked by all for the sake of more profits.

Express yourselves naturally towards these Evil Tran groups and complain at them, hounding them as they do to people like us. These fake merchants of morality deliver the ideology that biological men can be real women and that we must agree with them because they say so.

Tell them that they have no right to ignore and dismiss, and walk over real women for the sake of a trans agenda to instate men as women. They are trying to eradicate the definition of a woman. They cancel people, and they wish to delete our rights to free speech.

This is our opinion for anyone who is a trans frightener (a person who supports men as women and cancel bullying culture).

This below is what should be emailed more or less to any trans celebrity or organisation that supports trans rights as if above women's rights based on distortions of truth, misleading virtue, signalling language.

You defend trans people as if most were legally female when facts prove most are legally male. **You** have the audacity to inform the public that men are women just because they identify as so. **You** encourage the cancellation of people's jobs and contracts by supporting wholehearted trans culture and their aggressive stance against people who do not agree that a man can be a woman. **You** undermine every woman and girl by supporting the idea that naked biological men can shower openly before them. Would **you** date a biological female known as a trans man? Have you ever showered naked next to a biological male known as a trans woman? Do **you** have no understanding of how deplorably intrusive such shower procedures are for women and young girls? And how this via people like **you** naturally targets Muslim and Jewish women who cannot be alone in spaces with biological men.

Explain exactly why **you** believe a man can be a woman. If **you** believe because the law says so, then explain the law that overrides the criteria for the definition of a woman not being a biological entity.

If **you** are so lawful, why do **you** say things like trans women are women? When over 90% of them do **not** have a legally affirming gender recognition certificate, in other words, they are legally male like all normal men. Explain why **you** support the closing down of people like JK Rowling and Maya Forstater as if they cannot have free speech to voice opinions that men cannot be women. Did **you** not know that Maya Forstater was informed by the high court that it is our human right to voice our opinions, even if it upsets other people like **you**?

We put it to **you** that **you** are a disgrace to the majority of UK citizens, especially women who are being forced to lose the definition of themselves because people like **you** support the raping of our intellectual right to define a woman. We believe that **you** should be cancelled from society, be it at work or in a contract, because **you** do not represent the majority of women in society; **you** represent oppression and the closing of free speech by obnoxious public statements that afford you further powers to manipulate a social agenda against other fair-minded citizens who share opposing views.

I, like others, intend to encourage people with my sort of views to not support **you** in your political agendas by not buying your products and by telling as many people as possible to do the same. **You** have lost the right to be supported because you are part of an insidious movement of people in the UK who are supporting the closure of free speech via bullying cancelling tactics that support men who say they are women.

What exactly is **your** definition of a woman? Mine is along the scientific logical line that, in principle, a woman has the biological X and X chromosomes that a man does not. Women are the ones that give birth and are generally easily recognizable as women when dressed, especially when naked in a shower room. The men that infiltrate these spaces are not women and should go back to their own shower rooms based upon the way society has always decided these matters by male sex or female sex. Currently, if a person is non-binary, they can technically enter women's spaces when forced to choose between male and female. By some other ridiculous logic, non-binaries are sometimes asked to use the disabled facility if they refuse to choose a gender preference, which is their right.

Overall, this is the supplanting of fair and equal rights, especially for women, but it impacts dramatically on all men as well, because impractically, men are arguably women unless it is known for certain they are not. This has deep felt social knock-on effects because how do we socialize and decide who is a woman and a man in a transgender world? By law, we are not supposed to ask a person if they have a gender recognition certificate. So suddenly, we are all forced to exist within socially interactive contexts where any person could be anything.

We cannot conclude when a man is a woman because some men do not dress like women to clearly show they identify as women. This also means that every woman we meet might be a self-identified man. Suddenly, this intrusive structure of reasoning is infringing on everyone's right to make natural comments, enquiries and communications, as we have always known. We are being penned in with laws and rules, all articulated by people who are educated and continuously lobby politicians. As if they can work out what is best for how humans should behave when, really, we have developed these social norms over centuries through our daily interactions.

If we cannot decide a man or a woman based on appearances, we would need to ask questions to establish facts or skirt around the issue, which adds up to a cancellation of women and men in understood awareness and social norms and the way for humans to conduct social interaction in the habitual way we have done so historically. If the basic understanding of a man and a woman is lost, we lose a natural mechanism of communication and the feeling of the self to express our niceties.

In other words, these trans rules informing society of how to behave as social norms mean that Stonewall has the audacious right to tell the lesbian community to sleep with men. And people like **you** are defending this insidious movement that has infiltrated the university population to engage in hate speech against the majority of people in society.

A bunch of half-educated 18- to 25-year-olds are laying down the law via protests and social media hounding, and many people in the media, corporations, politics, and celebrities support them. **You** represent the overthrow of free speech and a sense of justice to speak as one finds. **You** represent the issuing of new ways for everyone to accept and copy as part of their personalities and character, which in itself is as repulsive and intrusive as you can get. Do you own people's souls and have the right to dictate to them?

Enough is enough; you should receive the pushback and political, financial, and social losses that you deserve for not representing women in society. **You** are on the target list that encourages fellow citizens to openly question you and boycott your social policies or products you earn a living from or are socially accepted and understood through.

We find **your** opinions invasive, intrusive, dictatorial, and certainly lacking any respect for the rights of women. We stick by JK Rowling, Posie Parker, Kathleen Stock, Maya Forstater, Helen Joyce, and women like them who defend women's rights, and we encourage no one to stick by **you**.

If you want a copy of that declaration in an email to you so that you can resend it on to where you wish just email:
realwomanorg@gmail.com

Chapter 8

Goodbye

Get the trans community out of the opposite sex spaces is the message here, where the law must be changed. If that law is not changed, stay there, as that is the legal right. The matter is as simple as that. This matter will be resolved by referendum eventually, or the UK society will wane into a woke spectacle where people lose understanding as to what it really means to support minority rights as they pose their morality to supporting a wish list from every minority group. Power to the majority of people has become power to the educated classes working in politics, media, corporations, the public sector, education, and celebrities with a decent enough following. I wouldn't mind if they worked arguments out to a sophisticated level of understanding consistent with supporting the majority of people, but most do not. Instead, they opt for convenient virtue signalling in a blanket response where everything is rounded off as a public statement that they 'support trans rights.' These people do not represent progression, and the majority of people in the UK. They maintain a culture based on how they think, aggressively expressing opinions through their power base. This often involves a monetisation of those opinions or an increase in power for them. Generally, people with media attention if succeeding to be popular have greater success selling their image, service, or product as a result of those modern-day liberal opinions. They actually calculate these advantages for presentation in public forums, which often means they have a fabricated, calculating personality and often hold sickly opinions against the majority rule. This does not mean these opinions are invalid, just that they have become a trend in how to establish oneself publicly and establish power.

It is all too easy to play to the crowd of one's choice or indulge in simplistic thinking. No single group has all the answers, but in democracy, it is often best that the majority view maintains the majority of power; if not, we have to concede that the minority view must maintain the majority of power. Take your choice is my observation for you, but at least be aware that is the choice. These power plays, including transgender rights displayed through different mediums, are fair and unfair given certain definitions. Sometimes the majority must adjust to aid the minority per se. And sometimes we rely on the new minority view to educate the majority of us. Such is a great example of progressive leadership and sophisticated development for human culture. But such an agency or mechanism relies on greater skill and intelligence to reap great and good ends; it must not succumb to lazy-styled thinking in order to maintain its power; it must possess the virtue to commit suicide and lose that power if need be for the sake of what is best. Understood without further analysis, sometimes what is best or what is the truth is not a thing that can be worked out; it is a thing of choice that is often self-suiting to one's thinking. Once so, I believe it should then favour the majority and not the minority. In regards to trans rights, some of it is right and some of it is wrong. It should not be a blanket response to support all those so called rights because of the reasons I have focused on throughout this book. Don't be a lazy-thinking human, and if caught out as if seemingly incorrect, adjust. If not, society creates hardships for itself. The hardships pressing upon us at present in regards to trans powers and their exponents of truth, like the Labour Party, celebrities, or other powerful organisations, are that they have altered too much without first seemingly asking and checking with the majority in UK society. Please think about this and decide if it is right.

To recap and clarify . . . here is some essential logic for you to consider in relation to the books content. I have made it clear that the thinking and emotions of men can access the emotions and thinking of women; there is not a mechanism infringing the activity in human brains to stop any of us from thinking and feeling a certain selection of ways open to all of us. If so, all that is left to separate men from women is some biological aspect.

Most of the time, men and women use the same emotional and cognitive ranges to live their lives; so are they men or women on such occasions, or simply humans? When we do differentiate, like I might think of beer football and male clothes, I could easily transform my ways into the thinking and feeling of a woman for cooking, dresses, and flowers, but this does not magically recreate me into a woman. But let us suppose, by consensus of the political academia community, a man who thinks like a woman or is distressed at not being a woman physically is defined as a woman and can enter women's spaces; under no circumstances of argument are there more than two sexes regardless of all the varieties from the flukes in nature that occur involving hormones, chromosomes, and types of anatomy outcomes where some men can look feminine and females masculine. The combination effects are mere routes to a conclusion where a sex is male or female and is assigned based around the ability of the human to produce sperm or eggs, which in turn tells biologists what role the female and male will play, whereby the female will give birth. In rare examples called intersex type, a sort of half-and-half hybrid, the so-called masculine lookalike may have a penis and vagina but give birth; this might classify him as female by the outcome produced from all the mixes he or she is, but even though this is rare, it does not alter the logic of the biological method to insist on a two-sex system.

As understood in biology and UK law, we only have two sexes: male and female. Non-binary (no-sex gender identity or mixed-sex gender identity) does not exist. The arguments in law and political minds and their forcing upon social behaviour say that outside of biology, men can be women; it does not state whatsoever that a man can change his sex, only that he can change how he perceives himself to be, from which politicians support that claim.

People like me do not support that claim because we simply do not agree that biology does not count in classifying what a woman is. For us, a woman in principle has the ability through the womb to give birth. If not there is no human race. I believe this sensory distinction has evolved through time as a natural mechanic in the brain and cannot be overridden by fancy-articulated ideas contrary to that perception and human skill to spot a potential partner or type of body for sex. Given that we show 100 photos of men and 100 of women to any of us, the brain will produce evidence that we each clarify men from women via an automatic response that conscious control will not be able to cancel.

I also believe that people who argue for trans rights; that men can be women, if given a lie detector test and asked if the picture of a man dressed as a woman is a woman, they will show signs of lying if they reply that it is a woman. I challenge the transgender community and all its followers, especially at any university, to this test. Some will pass as telling the truth, but most will be revealed for the frauds they are in some seat of awareness, and show themselves to be lying. Although I have to say in this context, it may not be a lie, but rather that the brain and a part of conscious awareness are signalling the power of the ability for humans to concede they recognize the biological man as a man and not a woman just because he wears a dress. I would be totally shocked to find that much above 20% pass such a lie detector test that says a man in a dress is a woman. The figure could arguably turn out to be a lot lower, much to the embarrassment of the transgender community, I am sure. But that is the price of lying to yourself and to others, so it is I challenge you all, especially those in academia.

Added to this, consider the two ways to become a woman according to the UK political legal sphere, and remember that if this is all there is to being a woman, then any woman reading this should not think of herself as anything special whatsoever: the state argues that people can be medically treated so that men can become women as a principle of law as the end result of their frame of argument. This is profoundly misleading and arguably laughable, where we see an example of well-managed theories from the academic quarter officializing sex change managed through their self-ordained power. In reality, it is the medical and legal professions appraisal of people who, via the introduction of a process, become the other sex via technical discount, by which the entry to being a woman from a man is really made via an intellectualized technical clerical process and not much more.

Meanwhile, many people assume (quite wrongly) that the medical profession has administered all the latest technical surgeries or chemicals that magically legitimize female status in some pull of logic or that the man concerned has undergone a psychological proof test where it can be shown that on many counts, this man is clearly a woman psychologically and deserves the status of a woman. In other words, many people assume that some carefully worked-out set of principles from highly intelligent professionals have been formulated that make it reasonable to say a man can be a woman based on these objective facts. When really the whole process is metered out based upon intensions from the man that do not even have to be upheld but once promised will transform him into female status via this medical legal process, whereby the official medical legal way is for a man to register with his doctor and then go to a gender dysphoria clinic where later on a man may wish to take an operation to alter his penis into a vagina or hormones that grow breasts. This is an impressive effort if he does that. Few do.

However, there is a further catch in the process, and it means that a man can simply inform the official body of experts that he may one day take hormones or might not, he may alter his dress sense from male to female, and he may change his title from Mister to Miss. In other words, a person can explain that they feel like a woman, or that they do not like their male body and would prefer they had a female body and wish to identify as a woman, but they cannot quite muster the exact list of efforts available as a choice of action; in other words, they can promise they might make some of those alterations or not. You can promise yourself to be a woman as officially upheld by the medical, legal, and political synergies. After two years, men become legal women when a gender recognition certificate is handed to them. From which they can change the male sex status on the birth certificate to female.

Interestingly; the second-easiest method, chosen by nearly all trans people, does not involve any reference to any psychological or biological aspects at all, just that the person decides to identify as a woman. It is an act of free will, just as a woman might call herself Ms instead of Mrs, or Miss. It is a clerical action as much as anything else based on simple declarations to organisations to change their titles on things like a passport, driving license, or any accounts they might have. 90% of men who say they are women take this social transitioning route.

So by example here, I will magically change myself from a man into a woman within seconds, literally – 'I wish to be known as a woman.' As soon as I say that I am officially transitioning into a woman, I might later alter my document gender titles, buy myself a dress and makeup, and so make it very clear that I am a trans woman, use the female showers and toilets, and join any exclusive women's only clubs, as I have the right, for all intents and purposes, to be treated with female legal status. The law allows me that right; all I cannot do is change my birth certificate to female, which means if I marry at a church, I would be married as a man.

There is no lawful testing process to confirm entry to womanhood when it comes to socially transitioning; there is no definitive set of rules and regulations that have to be met. It is as simple as a female changing her title from Miss to Ms or Mrs. We as a society would never have believed this or allowed it had we been asked; so one of the grounds for a referendum is an argument that politicians have not represented UK society as UK members would have expected, especially victimizing the population of Muslim and Jewish women where their religions dictate they cannot share confined spaces with biological men. They have fewer choices based on ideology, whereby if personal space rules of their religion are broken, family and friends will pressure them.

Since one law change in 2004, there has developed a cluster of infringements in UK culture allowing organisations to set the social agenda that we have to support trans rights if they say so to an extent and definition they set, which is basically a blanket response to every trans wish list. We all might agree to some trans rights, but not their every wish, and this includes the idea that they are real women when clearly biological men can never be real women if you include biological aspects. Just because 10% of them are legally accepted as women does not mean they are real women by our collective standards based on individual assessments from each of us.

We arrived at what we think is a woman naturally through how our cultures worked in tens of thousands of years, and in connection to how our brain biological systems carried genetic alterations over far greater amounts of time, we cannot reprogram non-conscious brain activity connected to identifying women via ideology. When we see a human body, the brain quickly and automatically processes the habits of thousands of generations imprinted as a survival tool in the brain, which includes the ability to spot a potential partner to have a sexual encounter with. We do not seek partners that do not interest us, and one resounding quality we identify is male and female. We carry this prejudice because it comes from a long line of human preferences. Once society attempts to fiddle with and alter this natural inclination and drive, it is a recipe for conflict because eventually people will realize they cannot naturally process information as political powers wish. All we can do is consciously modify it by lying, or at the very least, live with the feelings of unconscious conscious conflict – a sort of sickening feeling as we find ourselves fundamentally undermining our true natures. In other words, we are encountering an evil cultural phenomenon poisoning our wills and spirit of who we are.

Let us have a quick look at the sort of entangled thought process going on here.

What we seek as a female partner has a proviso: a woman with a biological woman's body, not a male body – filter the environment like this, or else end up with a woman that can be a biological man.

You might say that you simply think to look for a woman, not a trans woman. But a trans woman is a woman, is he not? Make up your mind here; in law he is female, you have to mentally view him as she, if the social condition you agree to is accurate, if not, ask why you do not mentally process him as a woman, and the answer is that the person is not a woman, and if so, then why the hell are we all pretending to ourselves in the media and political representations that he is a woman? Because we are frauds is one answer. Sort of sycophantic actions found from citizens in North Korea, where they all stand to clap and smile as if delighted citizens.

We have no right in a UK democracy to just accept or be forced to untangle all that mental baggage. But the youth in general are being brainwashed; they have to accept the truth in the situation that people have a human right to socially transition and create their own identity, and it must be accepted. Written up in rules and regulations, involving pages of paragraphs, the literal mind bending complex definitions of logic and rules to this ideology; it is an intellectual understanding of womanhood, not primal instinct. It carries no overriding objective proof and is accessed by men in a few seconds by saying to others that I wish to be known as a woman.

We cannot unpick all of this understood ideology in a fraction of a second for any of it to literally make clear sense in a real-life situation. We won't understand that complexity when looking for a partner choice; we will simply reject the pretend woman as a woman. This means we are being true to our natures as to what we believe instinctively to be a woman and rejecting the socially forced version. Then, when we get asked in any public social situation, we modify our answer and say yes, a man can be a woman via self-identification.

This trans dehumanising process collectively held across different organisations is the beginning of something far more sinister than just a human rights argument. If you do not get a feel for this now, you will at a later stage as we become surrounded by humans who have quite literally become a fraudulent sickly human specimen held up in a conscious ideology believing they are right when clearly they are deceiving themselves that man can be woman based on biology, psychology, and sociology pseudo arguments when really it is actually the selling out and attack on one of the greatest fundamental rights and instincts the human race developed within itself generation after generation. We are trashing more than just our culture and right to decide – we are killing a part of the thing inside that we are, as people feed the trans lie into themselves and then into other members of society. In the end, this becomes a deep and meaningful spiritual condition to fight for, where the more innately needed emotional and thoughtful qualities must be nurtured or die. When you live a lie, you die inside. But when you believe a lie, you actually do better as a survival entity found in evolution. It makes little difference to the child growing up because he or she might adjust to this new form of human processing, but it still remains that questions will remain unanswered as later cultures will still seek sexual biological male and female partners, fully rejecting the self-identity partner.

This indicates just how important we value the favoured male or female body as a desire to obtain it in a partnership. I argue that this reflects an innate evolutionary understanding that is not ideologically created but some acute sense of the value of the person to that individual based on biology: it is simply this distinction we call man or woman we understand as a thing we can share and experience biologically. All the intellectual and academic arguments about recreating women into some sophisticated psychic elements while rejecting their biological contents are not something any of us do when looking for a partner. Heterosexual men quite literally do not care one iota for the socially generated self-identity called gender female. And if we evolved through time using the biological mechanism of distinction that we encapsulate in our minds as man or woman, why would we change it to the psychology of a woman without the biological underpinnings?

Our woman who has stood the test of time has the accompanying psychology and personality of what we come to expect from her, but we all know she comes with a vagina and womb that can give us children. That is what woman means in human terms, and we know it. Academics have amazingly overcome these natural definitions and argued for mercy for self-identity people so that they are understood as legitimate women. In an act of intellectual will, they argued that biology does not count as a value to decide a woman. But I argue it is the value because heterosexual men and lesbians seem to seek this biological value, knowing full well that the person will have the corresponding personality and expression of a woman attached. All a trans person argues is that any man can have the personality of a woman and the experience of a woman, and that this should qualify them as a woman. Now heterosexual men and lesbians have to state that they only prefer women who are biological women and not women who are biological men.

In other words, there are two types of women. If not, what definition of a woman would you all like and then reflect in your actions? I can assure you all that none of you will choose a woman who is a biological man. It is a claptrap rat-intellectual concept, created by politically correct bureaucrats who are not really humanitarian but as plastic and contemptuous and business-like as you can possibly get. If you reading this do not get a feel for that, I can assure you that the plastic-coated manipulative corporate world has engulfed your thought process to just fall into their way of life, which is a way of law and order international agreement and worked out standards of virtue.

You should realize how easily any man can become a woman in the UK without any proof of biological or psychological depths or provable aspects that show one as being a woman.

In other words, the way to become a trans woman (who is then officially a woman) actually shows that real women hardly have a legitimate definition and protection as to what they are as any sort of value; they have quite literally been discarded into an intellectual political bin like a piece of common trash. This is why we must fight for a referendum and reclaim our rights to decide what a woman is. If not, know that any man is a woman if he says so. Know that politically you have no right to decide who men and women are based on biology. All men might be women and all women might be men, and you better accept that that applies to you because if not, some aspect of Evil Tran will attack you as it defends itself by the rules it made for itself, which are accepted within the selves of people in politics, media, education systems, and the rat pack that does not care for your individual will.

I despise the academic community in relation to this abomination of political logic and social upheaval that is acting to destroy freedom of speech, not the transgender community itself. Wear your dresses with pride as far as I am concerned. You might lose your toilets and showers but you won't lose your dress sense I am sure. Just as none of us should lose our sense of freedom of speech just because Evil Tran is on the loose killing freedom of speech and the dignity of women in showers.

Our gang must counter attack this cancel culture at every point on social media, television, interviews at work, articles written, university campuses, wherever and whenever. If the tranny brigade is going to force their ways and wills upon us, we are by far the bigger gang, then let us destroy their cultural hold by aggressive group actions that quite literally refuse to be told and sold-out to cheap shot lying and misleading claims that trans rights are human rights; a garbage rhetoric from elites like the Labour leader and others. No one is asking them to stop dressing and acting as they do. We are asking for social justice that it be decided by society members whether such men can ever be women via a referendum and not a tranny political dictate that is part of an Evil Tran phenomenon and academic mechanism to oppress the working class people of the UK into some sort of intellectualized prison.

Until the day when we rectify our errors via a referendum, I find the culture I am embedded in too weak and sycophantic, toxic and fraudulent, pretence and a parody. The earth is not flat; it is heating up, and COVID did kill millions. Women have vaginas and give birth to children and the entire human race. We should fight for that definition and way of being human: that a man is a man and a woman is a woman.

I wish you all well, and by that, I mean everyone, because, in spirit, we are all brothers and sisters.

Just remember that our sisters are real women and our brothers real men. Women will never be men in dresses. I dedicate this book to real women.

Chapter 9

A Transformative Tale for 6 Year Olds

White Teddy said to Brown Bunny, 'I don't know about you, but I feel like a change.'

Bunny said, 'Yes, we have been eating chocolate orange eggs for far too long; let's buy some white ones.'

So they went to the nearest corner shop, where a kind human with a fresh, happy smile called BiG X stood leaning against the counter.

BiG X only had one leg and was prone to toppling over. Without the friend known as Little x nearby to help out, BiG X might fall into the array of multicoloured rainbow sweets, milk and dark chocolates, some of which were square shaped, pear-shaped, and some were like a triangle. All were different, inclusive sizes. It is good to be all-inclusive.

White Teddy said, 'Hello, dear lady, please may we have some sweets of all kinds of colours and shapes because we don't want to leave any feeling left alone, unwanted, unused, unheard of, and confused.'

'Hello, Teddy, How are you today?'

'I am very well; thank you very much. It is Monday today, but we look forward to meeting all the other days of the week so that they can meet us to.'

'Good, because I am not known as dear lady or man or Miss or Mister . . . everyone calls me BiG X, and I exclude all common pronouns. Just so that I can make it easier for everyone to understand where I am not coming from.'

'Oh . . . thank you for letting me and Bunny know. Is a pronoun a new kind of sweet or chocolate?'

'It could be either, it can be whatever you want, when you want, as you want,' said BiG X.

'In that case, we will have two of them, we fancy a change, we have surely eaten too many orange sweets, look I have orange-coloured spots on my forehead.'

'Yes, there are seven of them for each day of the week. And how wonderful that every blemish has a different shape and size. There is no such thing as a favourite shape or size, you know. And if you have one leg, that is as good as having no legs, three legs, or two,' said BiG X.

'My dog has four legs, and its name is Tiger,' said Teddy.

.

'Oh, how brilliant,' said BiG X, 'you see you have a tiger that is a dog, that may well meow like a cat, that walks on its hind legs like a human. It is called a bi-legged creature and is very welcome here.'

'My mother calls Tiger a dog,' said Teddy.

'Yes, it might be a dog, but equally it might be a cat that is changing into a human that wishes to be known as – it, I am, a bit of both, and nothing,' said BiG X, and she handed Teddy a bag of sweets, each of which was a handy pronoun shape to know, in all types of chocolate flavours.

Teddy and Bunny left the shop and began to scoff their sweets. BiG X had not told them they were magic sweets and would change white Teddy into a brown Bunny and brown Bunny into a white Teddy.

White Teddy began to cry, 'Oh, I am in the most terrifying pain.'

Brown Bunny shouted, 'Oh, you are changing colour and the shape of your head looks ready to burst. There is a bump between your legs, and to make things worse, our school teacher, Judith, the 'one-eyed, they, that, here today gone tomorrow' is here or there. And will be very upset that we missed school. And then, very upset that she didn't give, not being upset, an equal chance also.'

'Hello, Bunny and Teddy, are you ready to fly on the magic carpet to the moon in the sky? Late at night before the dawn, and when you return, be a Teddy and a Bunny instead of a Bunny and a Teddy?'

Teddy and Bunny nodded their heads (because to do so would save them a bit of a mouthful) held hands, and took to the darkening sky, fully transformed as they scoffed those magical bags of sweets. The very next day, Teddy and Bunny went to the sweet shop.

'Hello Teddy, hello Bunny, how are you today?' said BiG X, with a rather deep masculine voice. 'Do you like my multi-coloured dress?' BiG X did a twirl, as the disfigured Teddy and melted Bunny stood to observe BiG X's trick and treats.

'I'm actually Bunny, formerly known as Teddy. This is my friend Teddy, formerly known as Bunny. We have gone to the cult moon and back and changed ourselves.'

'Well done, you that is known as Bunny but was formerly known as Teddy.'

'Could we have the same again?' said Bunny, who was formerly known as Teddy.

BiG X smiled, did a twirl on its one leg, and quickly produced an array of sweets, chocolates, and magical enchantments all in two bags, all ready to be eaten. BiG X handed a bag to each of them.

Off they skipped, out the shop, and down the road they went, fully transformed. As they passed their school, they waved and said that they were off to the magic half-moon in the sky and would be back tomorrow. All the bunnies and teddies waved to their friends. Judith, the evil, wicked school teacher, smiled as she watched her magic spell alight the darkening sky. Like a puff of smoke, it shone bright and made a noise like a popsicle being whistled through by fire rockets.

Down below were their good older friends Daniel and Emma, who were waving and smiling and setting an example for all to follow.

The next day, BiG X awaited in a new frilly, rainbow-colored dress.

'Oh, my little transitioned darlings, how are we today? Would you like a bag of sweets?'

'No thanks,' said Teddy, who was formerly Bunny and formerly again Teddy. 'We watched a video by a kind lady called Posie Parker. On it, she showed us a magic trick for how to de-transition. If I ate the sweets for Bunny, I would turn back into Teddy, like Hey-Presto. We swapped the sweet bags around that you gave us, and when we got to the moon, we ate them and changed back into our real Teddy and Bunny bodies.'

BiG X did a twirl so fast he kept spinning and spinning until he fell over into a bump, a clump, a heap, and a thump. With no way to socially influence he fell rather sick.

Teddy and Bunny laughed and giggled, skipped and danced, did two summersaults, and took their chance. They ran into the arms of Posie Parker, who flew them to the school, where she cast a magic spell over that evil witch, Judith, who disappeared in a puff of magical green smoke. As she went, she farted, and all the teddies and bunnies could be heard to laugh.

JK Rowling, the new head teacher, came out to greet all the teddies and bunnies. She, that Miss, that MS, that Mrs., that real woman with fine legs and a smouldering smile, declared to Teddy and Bunny, 'Tell your classmates the travels you have been on.'

And for the next hour, Teddy and Bunny told all the tales about the silly adults and their tales about the friendly sweetshop where BiG Evil X had tricked them into changing all the beautiful things they were.

JK Rowling asked Teddy and Bunny, 'What advice do you offer to all the Bunnies and Teddies?'

And Teddy and Bunny spoke together in unison, 'Don't take sweets from white fantasy land educated parents; for they do not have your best interests at heart; they only care to look good and fulfil their weakness as lame intellectual moral guides.'

And all the Teddies and all the Bunnies hopped, danced, laughed, and giggled, and Emma and Daniel walked crying as they returned back to the school of hard knocks at average white-middle-class university-educated-land, where all funny-shaped academic assholes come from. Ha, ha, ha to you!

. . . And fuck you all in the Tranny mind-warping transitioning-kids-society; shame on you, boohoo sharks in goldfish clothing!

And all the children in all the schools shouted, 'JK Rowling and Posie Parker are our heroes.'

The END

And they all lived happily ever after.

Glossary

anti-tran Dalek – an entity that wishes to 'exterminate' the reign and rights of transgenders.

bitch-men-slags – men who sell out all men and women as if the opposite sex.

bitch-women-slags – women who sell out all men and women as if the opposite sex.

catch tranny 22 – situation whereby Human Rights protecting a person's sex as a thing not to be discriminated against is included in the idea that a person's gender identity perceived as female is also protected.

cisgender – a woman psyche in a woman body / a perfectly normal human.

Cissy Bitch Gang – JK Rowling, Maya Forstater, Posie Parker, Kathleen Stock and Helen Joyce.

corporate intellectualization – intellectual powers naturally connected as if a corporation.

cult of trans – the brain dead followers who worship trans rights and all its beliefs.

feel free – the ability to feel as you choose by design and selection of choices to design one's own emotional reflective actions via continual reinforcement.

femmephobic – lesbians prejudiced against trans women.

Frank theory: bits and pieces of logic theory mish mashed together into a whole as Frankenstein was before he walked.

intellectual and moral trashcan – the lie that some men are women, and we are moral to let men in women's shower rooms.

illegal tran – tran without a gender certificate.

intellectual gassing – skilled academic arguments tying people up in rules and regulations.

Judas Butlers – the political classes that betrayed society women's rights and decency.

legal tran – tran person with a gender certificate.

man-bitch – man / transgender woman.

misgendering – calling someone mister if they wish to be called Miss.

non-entity – a person who mimics transwomen in a 'does not exist' sexual category as a joke.

psychological-woman – transwoman.

pre trans – showing signs of being a trans person yourself but not knowing it.

sign flashers – we support trans rights and like to look good doing so.

Social Nazism – ideas from elites and the educated classes ordering people how to behave.

social tranny agenda – how cisgenders must behave dancing around trans rights and wishes.

tranny land – a cosmic view of transgender reality and all it brings in its rich diversity of language which in itself is a cult fashion.

tran Nazi state – a dictatorship fulfilling a trend to challenge and alter perceived historical reality based on will to argue.

tranny academic state – academics who argue ordering and instructing society to be all inclusive to trans people when not all inclusions are anything to do with human rights but merely subjective opinions.

trans intellectual pseudo reality – misleading or lying conclusions and statements by tran academics and university intellectuals especially.

trans tarts – trans friendly academics especially fraudulent for cash and university positions.

tranny driver – a trans person or cisgender who steers and argues and represents trans rights wholeheartedly above others in society.

TIS: Trans Ideological Spectrum.

trans rights – the right to exist as we all do without prejudice against them to do so.

trans logic – men can be women and we must not under any circumstances see things differently.

tranny-retard – a trans belief so absurd they must be a mentally ill to believe it.

trans-woe-women – trans internal wish and view that real women are woe.

trans hater fans – trans people who love to hate you as entertainment.

trans Lives Matter – making the Trans issue psychologically similar to black lives matter.

trans lie rhetoric – misleading venues of logic whereby they twist truth or manage lies into their own sounding truth.

transphobe – someone who disregards trans people because they do not understand them as they should be understood.

trannyization – the ability to enforce fear of losing job and social status upon people.

Tranny Hogwarts – people who follow celebrities in the cause for or against trans people.

trans frightener – a person who supports men as women and cancel bullying culture.

tranny brigade – the people in all sorts of organizations who support trans people at the expense of women's rights.

tranny knickers – mindfully vacant enough to fit more intellectual trans bollocks in.

trans brigade – those that as a group act in a coherency and union to stand for trans.

trans-shebang – the movement the ideology the actions the wishes the fight for rights to be accepted as women.

tranny state – we must do as trans people and their think tank of followers say and request.

tranny train – a system of virtue signaling whereby its gang members artfully position themselves as custodians of societal norms and values.

Milton Keynes UK
Ingram Content Group UK Ltd.
UKHW052030250324
439790UK00003B/4